Mastering MATLAB: A Comprehensive Journey Through Coding and Analysis

Kameron Hussain and Frahaan Hussain

Published by Sonar Publishing, 2024.

MASTERING MATLAB: A COMPREHENSIVE JOURNEY THROUGH CODING AND ANALYSIS

First edition. January 25, 2024.

ISBN: 979-8224671748

Written by Kameron Hussain and Frahaan Hussain.

Table of Contents

1. Tall Arrays

2. Datastore and Parallel Computing

3. Database Connectivity

4. Memory-Mapped Files

5. Distributed Computing

Section 17.4: Distributed Computing and MATLAB

1. Parallel Computing Toolbox

2. Parallel Data Processing

3. Distributed Computing on Clusters

4. Task Synchronization

5. Scaling and Load Balancing

Section 17.5: Performance Optimization Strategies

1. Vectorization

2. Preallocation

3. Memory Management

4. Algorithm Selection

5. Parallel Computing

6. Profiling and Benchmarking

7. Mex Files

8. Optimized Libraries and Toolboxes

4. GitHub and Version Control

5. ReadMe Files

6. Documentation Generators

7. Online Platforms and Forums

8. Licensing and Permissions

9. Collaboration and Contribution Guidelines

10. Update and Maintain

Section 19.3: Community and Online Resources

1. MATLAB Central

2. Stack Overflow

3. GitHub

4. MATLAB Documentation and Tutorials

5. Online Courses and MOOCs

6. YouTube Tutorials

7. LinkedIn Groups

8. Research Papers and Journals

9. Contribute to Open Source

10. MathWorks Support

Section 19.4: Career Opportunities and MATLAB Certification

Career Opportunities

3. Computational Chemistry and Materials Science

4. Climate Modeling and Environmental Studies

5. Personalized Medicine

6. Space Exploration and Astronomy

7. Cybersecurity and Data Privacy

8. Fusion of AI and Scientific Computing

9. Human-Machine Collaboration

10. Educational Advancements

Section 20.3: MATLAB in Space Exploration and Astronomy

1. Mission Planning and Navigation

2. Data Analysis and Image Processing

3. Simulating Celestial Phenomena

4. Telescope Control and Automation

5. Gravitational Wave Analysis

Section 20.4: The Role of MATLAB in Sustainable Technologies

1. Renewable Energy Systems

2. Electric Vehicle (EV) Development

3. Sustainable Agriculture

4. Environmental Monitoring

5. Sustainable Building Design

Section 20.5: MATLAB and the Advancement of AI and Machine Learning

1. Deep Learning Frameworks

2. Data Preparation and Preprocessing

3. Machine Learning Model Development

4. Explainable AI and Interpretability

5. Deployment and Integration

6. AutoML and Hyperparameter Tuning

7. Research and Innovation

Chapter 1: Introduction to MATLAB

1.1 Understanding the MATLAB Environment

IN THIS SECTION, WE will delve into the fundamental aspects of the MATLAB environment. MATLAB, which stands for Matrix Laboratory, is a high-level programming language and interactive environment designed primarily for numerical computing, data analysis, and visualization. It is widely used in various scientific, engineering, and academic disciplines due to its versatility and powerful capabilities.

What is MATLAB?

AT ITS CORE, MATLAB is built around the concept of matrices and arrays. It excels in performing matrix and vector operations, making it a valuable tool for linear algebra, numerical analysis, and scientific computing. MATLAB also provides a vast library of built-in functions and toolboxes that simplify complex tasks in various domains.

Launching MATLAB

TO GET STARTED WITH MATLAB, you typically open the MATLAB application. Upon launch, you'll be greeted by the MATLAB Command Window, where you can directly enter and execute MATLAB commands. Additionally, there is the MATLAB Editor, where you can create and edit scripts and functions, making it easier to develop larger and more organized programs.

% Example of launching MATLAB and performing a simple calculation

```
x = 5;

y = 10;

result = x + y;

disp(result);
```

The MATLAB Workspace

ONE OF THE KEY FEATURES of MATLAB is its workspace, which is essentially a storage area for variables and data. You can create, manipulate, and analyze data within the workspace. The workspace provides a graphical interface where you can view and manage your variables.

Command Line vs. Scripting

IN MATLAB, YOU HAVE two primary ways to interact with the environment: the command line and scripting. The command line is useful for quick calculations and testing individual commands. On the other hand, scripting allows you to write and save a sequence of MATLAB commands in a script file, making it convenient for repetitive or complex tasks.

```
% Example of a simple MATLAB script

% This script calculates the area of a rectangle

length = 5;

width = 3;

area = length * width;

fprintf('The area of the rectangle is %.2f square units.\n', area);
```

Help and Documentation

MATLAB PROVIDES EXTENSIVE documentation and help resources. You can access the documentation from the Help menu or by using the help function followed by the function or topic you want to learn more about. Additionally, the MATLAB community and online forums are valuable sources of information and assistance when you encounter challenges in your MATLAB journey.

This section has provided an overview of the MATLAB environment, including its core concepts, interface, and basic interaction methods. In the subsequent sections of this chapter, we will explore the history and evolution of MATLAB, its basic syntax and operations, and how it compares to other programming languages. Understanding these fundamentals will pave the way for a deeper exploration of MATLAB's capabilities.

1.2 History and Evolution of MATLAB

THE HISTORY OF MATLAB is a fascinating journey that traces its origins to the late 1970s. MATLAB was initially developed by Cleve Moler, a mathematician and computer scientist, as a tool for his students at the University of New Mexico to simplify numerical computations. Over the years, it has evolved into a powerful and widely used programming language and environment. Let's explore the key milestones in the history of MATLAB.

Early Beginnings

IN THE LATE 1970S, Cleve Moler created MATLAB (short for "Matrix Laboratory") as a Fortran-based software package to assist his students with linear algebra computations. MATLAB's initial purpose was to provide an accessible and efficient means of performing matrix calculations, which were prevalent in scientific and engineering applications.

```
% Early MATLAB code for matrix multiplication

A = [1, 2; 3, 4];

B = [5, 6; 7, 8];

result = A * B;

disp(result);
```

MATLAB's Commercialization

IN THE EARLY 1980S, Moler and his colleagues rewrote MATLAB in C to improve its performance and portability. In 1984, MathWorks, a company founded by Jack Little and Steve Bangert, was established to commercialize MATLAB. This marked the beginning of MATLAB's widespread adoption in academia and industry.

Growth and Expanding Capabilities

MATLAB CONTINUED TO grow in popularity due to its expanding capabilities. The addition of toolboxes and libraries for various domains, such as signal processing, image processing, and control systems, made MATLAB an indispensable tool for researchers and engineers.

```
% Example of using a MATLAB toolbox for signal processing

% Filtering a noisy signal

signal = randn(1, 100);

filtered_signal = filter(b, a, signal);
```

```
plot(signal, 'b');

hold on;

plot(filtered_signal, 'r');
```

Graphical User Interface (GUI)

IN THE MID-1990S, MATLAB introduced its graphical user interface (GUI), making it more user-friendly and accessible to individuals who were not necessarily proficient in programming. The GUI allowed users to interact with MATLAB through menus, buttons, and visual tools.

Advancements in Parallel Computing

AS COMPUTATIONAL NEEDS grew, MATLAB evolved to support parallel computing and GPU acceleration. This allowed users to harness the power of multi-core processors and GPUs for faster and more efficient computations.

```
% Example of parallel computing in MATLAB

% Parallelizing a loop for increased performance

parfor i = 1:100

result(i) = expensive_function(i);

end
```

Modern Era and Beyond

IN RECENT YEARS, MATLAB has continued to adapt to emerging technologies and trends. It has expanded its support for data science, machine learning, and artificial intelligence, making it a versatile platform for a wide range of applications.

This section has provided a brief overview of the history and evolution of MATLAB, highlighting its transformation from a simple matrix computation tool to a comprehensive programming language and environment. MATLAB's journey showcases its enduring relevance in various fields of science and engineering. In the following sections, we will delve deeper into the core aspects of MATLAB, including its basic syntax, operations, and how it compares to other programming languages.

1.3 Basic Syntax and Operations

IN THIS SECTION, WE will explore the basic syntax and fundamental operations in MATLAB. Understanding the syntax is crucial as it forms the foundation for writing MATLAB code effectively.

MATLAB Syntax

MATLAB'S SYNTAX IS designed to be both intuitive and expressive. Commands are typically written in a way that resembles natural language, making it easier for users to convey their intentions. Statements and expressions are separated by semicolons or line breaks, and MATLAB is case-sensitive.

```
% Example of MATLAB syntax

a = 5; % Assigning the value 5 to variable 'a'

b = a * 2; % Performing a simple multiplication
```

Variables and Assignments

IN MATLAB, YOU CAN create variables and assign values to them. Variable names are case-sensitive and can consist of letters, numbers, and underscores. It's a good practice to choose meaningful variable names to enhance code readability.

```
% Variable assignments in MATLAB

x = 10; % Assigning a numeric value to 'x'

message = 'Hello, MATLAB!'; % Assigning a string to 'message'
```

Basic Operations

MATLAB SUPPORTS VARIOUS mathematical operations, including addition, subtraction, multiplication, and division, both for scalars and arrays. These operations can be performed directly in the command window or within scripts and functions.

```
% Basic arithmetic operations in MATLAB

a = 10;

b = 5;

addition_result = a + b;

subtraction_result = a - b;

multiplication_result = a * b;

division_result = a / b;
```

Comments

COMMENTS ARE ESSENTIAL for code documentation and understanding. In MATLAB, you can add comments using the '%' symbol. Comments are ignored by MATLAB when executing code and are only meant for human readers.

```
% This is a single-line comment in MATLAB
```

```
%{
This is a multi-line comment
that spans multiple lines
%}
```

Built-in Functions

MATLAB COMES WITH A vast library of built-in functions and toolboxes, which significantly simplify complex tasks. You can call these functions directly in your code. For example, MATLAB provides functions for mathematical operations, data analysis, and visualization.

```
% Using a built-in function to calculate the sine of an angle
angle = pi/4; % 45 degrees
sine_value = sin(angle);
```

Displaying Results

TO VIEW THE RESULTS of your calculations or display messages, you can use the disp and fprintf functions. disp is used to show values, and fprintf allows you to format and display text and numerical values.

```
% Displaying results using 'disp' and 'fprintf'
result = 42;
disp(result); % Display the result
fprintf('The result is %d.\n', result); % Display with formatting
```

Scripting and Functions

IN ADDITION TO WORKING in the command window, you can write MATLAB scripts and functions to organize your code and perform more complex tasks. Scripts are sequences of MATLAB commands saved in .m files, while functions are reusable blocks of code with defined inputs and outputs.

```
% Example of a simple MATLAB script

% This script calculates the area of a circle

radius = 3;

area = pi * radius^2;

fprintf('The area of the circle is %.2f.\n', area);
```

MATLAB's basic syntax and operations serve as the building blocks for more advanced programming and data manipulation. In the upcoming sections of this chapter, we will dive deeper into control structures, loops, and functions, enabling you to create more sophisticated MATLAB programs for various applications.

1.4 MATLAB vs. Other Programming Languages

IN THIS SECTION, WE will compare MATLAB to other programming languages and discuss its unique characteristics and advantages. Understanding how MATLAB differs from other languages can help you make an informed decision about when and why to use MATLAB for specific tasks.

High-Level vs. Low-Level Languages

ONE SIGNIFICANT DISTINCTION is that MATLAB is a high-level programming language, while languages like C, C++, or Assembly are considered low-level languages. High-level languages, including MATLAB, provide abstractions that hide the low-level details of hardware and memory management. This makes them easier to learn and use, as programmers can focus on problem-solving rather than dealing with memory allocation or hardware-specific instructions.

Numerical Computing Focus

MATLAB'S PRIMARY STRENGTH lies in numerical computing and mathematical operations. It is purpose-built for matrix and vector computations, making it highly efficient for mathematical modeling, data analysis, and scientific simulations. Other general-purpose languages may not have the same level of built-in support for numerical tasks, requiring additional libraries or custom code.

% Example of matrix multiplication in MATLAB

A = [1, 2; 3, 4];

B = [5, 6; 7, 8];

result = A * B;

Interactivity and Quick Prototyping

ONE OF MATLAB'S STANDOUT features is its interactive environment, which allows you to execute commands and see immediate results. This interactivity is beneficial for exploratory data analysis, algorithm development, and quick prototyping. Traditional compiled languages like C or Java may require writing and compiling code before seeing results, which can slow down the development process.

Extensive Toolbox Support

MATLAB PROVIDES A WIDE range of toolboxes and libraries that cater to various application domains. Whether you are working on image processing, signal analysis, control systems, or machine learning, MATLAB offers specialized toolboxes with pre-built functions and algorithms. In contrast, general-purpose languages often lack such domain-specific libraries, requiring you to implement these functionalities from scratch or find third-party packages.

```
% Using the Image Processing Toolbox for edge detection

image = imread('example.jpg');

edges = edge(image, 'Sobel');

imshow(edges);
```

Simplicity of Syntax

MATLAB'S SYNTAX IS designed to be user-friendly and expressive, resembling natural language. This simplicity makes it accessible to users with varying programming backgrounds. On the other hand, languages like C or Python may have more complex syntax and require a steeper learning curve.

Integration with Other Languages

WHILE MATLAB IS EXCELLENT for numerical computing, it may not always be the best choice for all programming tasks. For instance, web development or system-level programming is typically done in languages like JavaScript or C. However, MATLAB can be integrated with these languages using external interfaces, allowing you to leverage the strengths of both.

License and Cost

IT'S IMPORTANT TO NOTE that MATLAB is a commercial software with licensing fees, while many other programming languages and development environments are open-source and free to use. This cost consideration can be a factor when choosing the right tool for your project.

In summary, MATLAB's focus on numerical computing, interactive environment, extensive toolbox support, and user-friendly syntax make it a compelling choice for various scientific and engineering applications. However, the choice between MATLAB and other programming languages depends on the specific requirements of your project, your familiarity with the language, and budget constraints. MATLAB excels in its niche, but it's essential to evaluate alternatives when they better suit your needs.

1.5 Setting Up and Navigating the MATLAB Interface

IN THIS SECTION, WE will explore how to set up and navigate the MATLAB interface efficiently. Getting acquainted with the interface is essential for working effectively with MATLAB, whether you are a beginner or an experienced user.

Launching MATLAB

TO START USING MATLAB, you need to launch the MATLAB application on your computer. Depending on your operating system, you can typically find MATLAB in your program or application list. Once launched, you will be greeted by the MATLAB desktop environment.

MATLAB Desktop

THE MATLAB DESKTOP is the central hub for your MATLAB workflow. It consists of several key components:

1. **Command Window**: This is where you can enter MATLAB commands directly and see their results. It's a convenient way to perform quick calculations and test code snippets.
2. **Current Folder**: This panel shows the current working directory. You can navigate your file system, create folders, and manage your MATLAB files here.
3. **Editor**: The MATLAB Editor is a powerful tool for writing and editing scripts and functions. It provides syntax highlighting, code folding, and debugging features, making it ideal for larger coding tasks.
4. **Command History**: MATLAB keeps a record of previously executed commands in the Command History. You can recall and re-execute previous commands from this panel.
5. **Workspace**: The Workspace panel displays information about your variables, including their names, values, and sizes. It's useful for inspecting and managing your workspace.
6. **Current Folder Browser**: This browser allows you to explore your file system and access your MATLAB files, toolboxes, and functions conveniently.

Creating and Running MATLAB Scripts

TO CREATE A NEW MATLAB script, you can use the MATLAB Editor. Simply click on "File" in the MATLAB desktop menu and select "New Script." This will open a new script file in the Editor, where you can start writing and editing your code.

```
% Example of a simple MATLAB script in the Editor

% This script calculates the sum of two numbers

num1 = 5;

num2 = 7;

result = num1 + num2;

disp(result);
```

To run a script, you can click the "Run" button in the Editor or use the keyboard shortcut (F5 on Windows, Command+Enter on macOS). The script's output will appear in the Command Window.

MATLAB Documentation and Help

MATLAB PROVIDES EXTENSIVE documentation and help resources to assist you in your programming journey. You can access the documentation from the "Help" menu in the MATLAB desktop. The MATLAB documentation includes detailed information about functions, toolboxes, and programming concepts.

Customizing MATLAB

MATLAB OFFERS VARIOUS customization options to tailor the interface to your preferences. You can change the color scheme, adjust font sizes, and configure keyboard shortcuts. These options can enhance your productivity and make your MATLAB experience more comfortable.

Online Community and Resources

IN ADDITION TO THE built-in documentation, the MATLAB community is a valuable resource. You can find answers to questions, share knowledge, and seek assistance from fellow MATLAB users through online forums, blogs, and social media groups.

Closing MATLAB

WHEN YOU'RE FINISHED with your MATLAB session, you can close the application by clicking the "X" button in the MATLAB window's upper-right corner. MATLAB will prompt you to save any unsaved work and close the open files.

Understanding how to set up and navigate the MATLAB interface is the first step in becoming proficient with the software. As you explore MATLAB further, you will discover its rich set of features, including advanced programming capabilities, data analysis tools, and specialized toolboxes. The knowledge gained in this section will serve as the foundation for your MATLAB journey.

Chapter 2: Fundamental Programming Concepts

2.1 Variables and Data Types

IN THIS SECTION, WE will delve into the fundamental programming concepts in MATLAB, starting with variables and data types. Understanding how to work with variables and different data types is essential for any programming language, and MATLAB is no exception.

Variables in MATLAB

IN MATLAB, VARIABLES are used to store and manage data. A variable is essentially a named storage location that can hold different types of information. Variable names in MATLAB are case-sensitive and must begin with a letter, followed by letters, numbers, or underscores.

```
% Examples of variable declarations in MATLAB

x = 5; % Assigning an integer value to 'x'

message = 'Hello'; % Assigning a string to 'message'

value = 3.14; % Assigning a floating-point number to 'value'
```

Data Types

MATLAB SUPPORTS VARIOUS data types to represent different kinds of information. Some common data types in MATLAB include:

- **Numeric Types**: These include integers (int8, int16, int32, int64), floating-point numbers (single, double), and complex numbers (complex).

- **Strings**: Strings are sequences of characters enclosed in single or double quotes. MATLAB treats strings as arrays of characters.

- **Logical**: Logical data types represent true or false values and are used for logical operations.

- **Cell Arrays**: Cell arrays are versatile data structures that can hold data of different types and sizes.

- **Structures**: Structures allow you to group related data together under one variable name, with each piece of data referred to as a field.

Variable Assignment and Naming Conventions

WHEN ASSIGNING VALUES to variables, it's essential to follow naming conventions for clarity and readability. Descriptive variable names are preferred to convey the purpose of the variable. MATLAB's use of camel case (e.g., myVariableName) or underscores (e.g., my_variable_name) is common for variable naming.

```
% Example of meaningful variable naming

student_name = 'John Doe';

total_marks = 95;

is_passed = true;
```

Displaying Variables

TO VIEW THE VALUE OF a variable, you can use the disp function in MATLAB. It is particularly useful for displaying the contents of variables in the Command Window.

```
% Displaying variables using 'disp'

age = 30;

disp(age); % Display the value of 'age'
```

Clearing Variables

YOU CAN REMOVE A VARIABLE from the workspace using the clear function. This action deletes the variable and frees up memory.

```
% Clearing a variable from the workspace

clear age; % Remove the 'age' variable
```

Checking Variable Type

TO DETERMINE THE DATA type of a variable, you can use the class function. This function returns a string indicating the data type of the variable.

```
% Checking the data type of a variable

x = 42;

data_type = class(x);

disp(data_type); % Display 'double' since 'x' is a double-precision number
```

Understanding variables and data types is fundamental in MATLAB programming. As you proceed through this chapter, you will explore more programming concepts, including operators, expressions, control structures, and functions. These concepts will equip you with the knowledge and skills needed to write MATLAB code effectively and solve a wide range of problems in scientific and engineering applications.

2.2 Operators and Expressions

IN THIS SECTION, WE will explore operators and expressions in MATLAB. Operators are symbols that perform operations on variables and values, while expressions are combinations of operators and operands that result in a single value.

Arithmetic Operators

MATLAB SUPPORTS VARIOUS arithmetic operators for performing basic mathematical operations. These operators include addition (+), subtraction (-), multiplication (*), division (/), and exponentiation (^). You can use these operators to perform calculations involving numeric data types.

```
% Arithmetic operators in MATLAB

a = 10;

b = 3;

addition_result = a + b;

subtraction_result = a - b;

multiplication_result = a * b;

division_result = a / b;
```

```
exponentiation_result = a ^ b;
```

Relational Operators

RELATIONAL OPERATORS are used to compare values and return logical results. Common relational operators in MATLAB include equality (==), inequality (~= or ~=, which means "not equal to"), greater than (>), less than (<), greater than or equal to (>=), and less than or equal to (<=).

```
% Relational operators in MATLAB

x = 5;

y = 8;

is_equal = x == y; % Is x equal to y? (false)

is_not_equal = x ~= y; % Is x not equal to y? (true)

is_greater_than = x > y; % Is x greater than y? (false)

is_less_than = x < y; % Is x less than y? (true)

is_greater_or_equal = x >= y; % Is x greater than or equal to y? (false)

is_less_or_equal = x <= y; % Is x less than or equal to y? (true)
```

Logical Operators

LOGICAL OPERATORS ARE used to combine or manipulate logical values (true or false). Common logical operators in MATLAB include logical AND (&&), logical OR (||), and logical NOT (~). These operators are useful in controlling program flow and making decisions based on conditions.

```
% Logical operators in MATLAB
```

```
p = true;

q = false;

logical_and = p && q; % Logical AND (false)

logical_or = p || q; % Logical OR (true)

logical_not_p = ~p; % Logical NOT for p (false)

logical_not_q = ~q; % Logical NOT for q (true)
```

Assignment Operators

ASSIGNMENT OPERATORS are used to assign values to variables. The basic assignment operator in MATLAB is the equals sign (=). However, MATLAB also provides shorthand assignment operators that combine an operation with assignment, such as +=, -=, *=, /=, and ^=.

```
% Shorthand assignment operators in MATLAB

x = 10;

x += 5; % Equivalent to x = x + 5 (x is now 15)

x -= 3; % Equivalent to x = x - 3 (x is now 12)

x *= 2; % Equivalent to x = x * 2 (x is now 24)

x /= 4; % Equivalent to x = x / 4 (x is now 6)

x ^= 3; % Equivalent to x = x ^ 3 (x is now 216)
```

Operator Precedence

MATLAB FOLLOWS OPERATOR precedence rules to determine the order of operations in an expression. For example, multiplication and division have higher precedence than addition and subtraction. You can use parentheses to override the default precedence and control the order of evaluation.

% Operator precedence in MATLAB

result = 3 + 5 * 2; *% Multiplication has higher precedence (result is 13)*

result = (3 + 5) * 2; *% Parentheses override precedence (result is 16)*

Understanding operators and expressions is essential for performing calculations and making logical decisions in MATLAB. As you progress through your programming journey, you will use these fundamental concepts to create more complex algorithms and solve a wide range of problems.

2.3 Control Structures: If-Else, Switch-Case

IN THIS SECTION, WE will explore control structures in MATLAB, focusing on conditional statements such as if-else and switch-case. These control structures are essential for controlling the flow of a program and making decisions based on conditions.

Conditional Statements

CONDITIONAL STATEMENTS allow you to execute different blocks of code based on specified conditions. In MATLAB, the primary conditional statements are if-else and switch-case.

if-else Statements

THE if-else statement is used when you want to execute one block of code if a condition is true and another block if the condition is false. The basic syntax of an if-else statement in MATLAB is as follows:

```
if condition
% Code to execute if the condition is true
else
% Code to execute if the condition is false
end
```

Here's an example:

```
% Example of an if-else statement
age = 20;
if age >= 18
disp('You are an adult.');
else
disp('You are not yet an adult.');
end
```

switch-case Statements

THE switch-case statement is useful when you have multiple possible conditions to check. It allows you to specify different code blocks to execute based on the value of an expression. The basic syntax of a switch-case statement in MATLAB is as follows:

```
switch expression
case value1
% Code to execute if expression matches value1
```

case value2

% Code to execute if expression matches value2

otherwise

% Code to execute if expression matches none of the cases

end

Here's an example:

% Example of a switch-case statement

day = 'Wednesday';

switch day

case 'Monday'

disp('It''s the beginning of the week.');

case 'Wednesday'

disp('It''s the middle of the week.');

otherwise

disp('It''s another day of the week.');

end

Nested if-else Statements

YOU CAN NEST if-else statements inside each other to handle more complex conditions. This allows you to create multiple levels of conditional checks within your code.

% Example of nested if-else statements

```
temperature = 28;
if temperature > 30
disp('It''s hot outside.');
else
if temperature < 15
disp('It''s cold outside.');
else
disp('The weather is moderate.');
end
end
```

Logical Operators in Conditionals

CONDITIONAL STATEMENTS often involve logical operators (&& for logical AND, || for logical OR, ~ for logical NOT) to combine multiple conditions. These operators enable you to create more complex conditions for decision-making.

```
% Example of using logical operators in conditionals
grade = 85;
if grade >= 90 && grade <= 100
disp('You got an A.');
elseif grade >= 80 && grade < 90
disp('You got a B.');
```

```
elseif grade >= 70 && grade < 80
disp('You got a C.');
else
disp('You got less than a C.');
end
```

Using break and continue

INSIDE LOOPS (WHICH we will cover in a later section), you can use the break statement to exit the loop prematurely if a certain condition is met. Conversely, the continue statement is used to skip the rest of the current iteration and move to the next iteration of the loop.

Control structures like if-else and switch-case are essential for creating programs that can make decisions and respond to different situations. They allow you to write code that behaves dynamically and adapts to changing conditions, making your MATLAB programs more versatile and powerful. As you continue your journey in MATLAB programming, you will frequently encounter these control structures in various applications.

2.4 Loops: For and While

IN THIS SECTION, WE will explore two essential types of loops in MATLAB: the for loop and the while loop. Loops allow you to repeat a set of instructions multiple times, which is a fundamental concept in programming.

The for Loop

THE for loop is commonly used when you know the number of iterations you want to perform in advance. It allows you to iterate over a sequence of values or elements, such as an array, and execute a block of code for each iteration. The basic syntax of a for loop in MATLAB is as follows:

```
for variable = range

% Code to execute for each value in the range

end
```

Here's an example of a for loop that iterates through a sequence of numbers:

```
% Example of a for loop

for i = 1:5

disp(['Iteration ', num2str(i)]);

end
```

In this example, the loop runs from i = 1 to i = 5, and the code within the loop is executed five times, displaying the iteration number each time.

The while Loop

THE while loop, on the other hand, is used when you want to repeat a block of code as long as a certain condition is true. It is suitable for situations where you may not know in advance how many iterations are needed. The basic syntax of a while loop in MATLAB is as follows:

```
while condition
% Code to execute while the condition is true
end
```

Here's an example of a while loop that continues to execute until a specified condition is no longer met:

```
% Example of a while loop
count = 1;
while count <= 3
disp(['Count is ', num2str(count)]);
count = count + 1;
end
```

In this example, the loop continues to execute as long as count is less than or equal to 3. The count variable is incremented with each iteration.

Loop Control Statements

INSIDE LOOPS, YOU CAN use loop control statements to modify the loop's behavior. Some commonly used loop control statements in MATLAB include:

- break: It allows you to exit the loop prematurely if a specific condition is met. For example, you can use break to terminate a loop when a particular value is found in an array.

- continue: It skips the current iteration and proceeds to the next iteration of the loop. This can be helpful when you want to skip some iterations based on a condition.

```
% Example of using 'break' and 'continue' in a loop

for i = 1:10

if i == 5

disp('Found the value 5.');

break; % Exit the loop

elseif i < 3

continue; % Skip iterations where i is less than 3

end

disp(['Iteration ', num2str(i)]);

end
```

Vectorization and Efficiency

MATLAB IS KNOWN FOR its powerful array operations, and whenever possible, it is recommended to utilize vectorized operations instead of explicit loops. Vectorization can lead to more efficient and faster code execution in MATLAB. However, loops are still necessary in situations where a task requires explicit iteration.

```
% Example of vectorized operation vs. explicit loop

data = [1, 2, 3, 4, 5];

% Vectorized operation to square each element
```

```
squared_data = data .^ 2;

disp(squared_data);

% Using a for loop to achieve the same result

squared_data_loop = zeros(1, numel(data)); % Preallocate the result array

for i = 1:numel(data)

squared_data_loop(i) = data(i) ^ 2;

end

disp(squared_data_loop);
```

In this example, both vectorized and loop-based approaches square each element in the data array. While vectorization is concise and efficient for this simple task, loops are essential for more complex scenarios.

Loops are powerful tools for automating repetitive tasks and handling dynamic situations in your MATLAB programs. As you gain experience, you will find creative ways to use loops to solve a wide range of problems efficiently.

2.5 Functions and Script Files

IN THIS SECTION, WE will explore the concept of functions and script files in MATLAB. Functions are reusable blocks of code that perform specific tasks, while script files are collections of MATLAB commands saved in a file for later execution. Both functions and script files are essential for structuring and organizing your MATLAB code.

Functions in MATLAB

FUNCTIONS ARE A FUNDAMENTAL concept in MATLAB and in programming in general. A function is a self-contained block of code that takes inputs, processes them, and returns outputs. Functions allow you to encapsulate specific functionality, making your code more modular, readable, and reusable.

Creating Functions

TO CREATE A NEW MATLAB function, you typically define it in a separate .m file with the same name as the function. MATLAB functions follow a specific structure, including the function signature, input arguments, and output arguments. Here's an example of a simple MATLAB function:

```
% Example of a MATLAB function

function result = add_numbers(a, b)

% This function adds two numbers and returns the result

result = a + b;

end
```

In this example, we define a function called add_numbers that takes two input arguments (a and b) and returns their sum as the output.

Calling Functions

ONCE YOU HAVE DEFINED a function, you can call it from the MATLAB Command Window or from other functions or script files. To call a function, you simply provide the necessary input arguments and capture the returned values.

```
% Calling the 'add_numbers' function

x = 5;

y = 3;

sum_result = add_numbers(x, y);

disp(['The sum of ', num2str(x), ' and ', num2str(y), ' is ', num2str(sum_result)]);
```

Built-in Functions

MATLAB COMES WITH A vast library of built-in functions that cover a wide range of tasks, from basic mathematical operations to advanced data analysis and signal processing. You can leverage these functions to perform complex operations without having to implement them from scratch.

Script Files in MATLAB

IN ADDITION TO FUNCTIONS, MATLAB allows you to create script files. A script file is a collection of MATLAB commands saved in a .m file that can be executed as a sequence of statements. Unlike functions, scripts do not take input arguments or return values, and they are executed in the current workspace.

Creating Script Files

CREATING A SCRIPT FILE in MATLAB is simple. You can open the MATLAB Editor, write your code, and save it with a .m extension. The code in a script file can include any valid MATLAB commands, and it will be executed when you run the script.

```
% Example of a MATLAB script file
```

disp('Hello, MATLAB!'); *% Display a message in the Command Window*

x = 10; *% Assign a value to the variable 'x'*

y = x * 2; *% Perform a calculation*

disp(['The value of y is ', num2str(y)]);

Running Script Files

TO RUN A SCRIPT FILE, you can simply type its name (without the .m extension) in the MATLAB Command Window and press Enter. MATLAB will execute the commands in the script file sequentially, and any output or changes to the workspace will be visible in the Command Window.

% Running the script file named 'my_script'

my_script

Function vs. Script

HERE ARE SOME KEY DIFFERENCES between functions and script files in MATLAB:

- **Input and Output**: Functions accept input arguments and return output values, while scripts do not. Scripts operate in the current workspace.
- **Modularity**: Functions promote modularity by encapsulating functionality, making code more organized and reusable. Scripts are often used for quick one-time tasks.

- **Namespacing**: Functions have their own variable workspace, known as a local workspace, which prevents conflicts with variables in the main workspace. Scripts share the same workspace as the Command Window.

- **Code Execution**: Functions are called explicitly, while scripts are executed by simply typing their name.

Both functions and script files have their roles in MATLAB programming, and choosing which one to use depends on the specific task at hand. Functions are excellent for creating reusable code components, while scripts are useful for running sequences of commands or interactive tasks.

As you continue your journey in MATLAB programming, you will frequently use functions and script files to organize your code effectively and perform various computational tasks.

Chapter 3: Advanced Programming Techniques

3.1 Writing Efficient MATLAB Code

IN THIS SECTION, WE will delve into the art of writing efficient MATLAB code. Efficient code is not only faster but also consumes fewer system resources, making it critical for large-scale data processing, simulations, and real-time applications. We will explore various techniques and best practices to optimize your MATLAB programs.

Vectorization

VECTORIZATION IS A fundamental concept in MATLAB that leverages its array-oriented capabilities. It involves performing operations on entire arrays or matrices rather than looping through individual elements. By vectorizing your code, you can take advantage of MATLAB's optimized algorithms and improve performance significantly.

Here's a simple example comparing a non-vectorized approach to a vectorized one for element-wise multiplication of two arrays:

```
% Non-vectorized approach

A = [1, 2, 3, 4];

B = [5, 6, 7, 8];

result = zeros(size(A));

for i = 1:length(A)

result(i) = A(i) * B(i);
```

```
end

% Vectorized approach

result_vectorized = A .* B;
```

In this example, the vectorized approach using the .* operator is not only more concise but also faster for large arrays.

Preallocation

WHEN WORKING WITH LARGE arrays or matrices, it's essential to preallocate memory for them whenever possible. MATLAB allows you to create empty arrays initially and then fill them with data. Preallocation prevents MATLAB from repeatedly reallocating memory during iterations, which can be time-consuming for large datasets.

```
% Preallocation example

n = 10000;

data = zeros(1, n); % Preallocate memory for 'data'

for i = 1:n

data(i) = i * 2;

end
```

Avoiding Global Variables

GLOBAL VARIABLES CAN lead to code that is challenging to maintain and debug. It's a good practice to avoid using global variables whenever possible. Instead, use function inputs and outputs to pass data between different parts of your code. This promotes modularity and makes it easier to test and reuse functions.

Profiling and Optimization

MATLAB PROVIDES PROFILING tools to analyze the performance of your code and identify bottlenecks. The Profiler can help you pinpoint which parts of your code consume the most time and resources. Once you identify performance-critical sections, you can focus on optimizing those specific areas.

```
% Using the MATLAB Profiler

profile on; % Start profiling

% Your code here

profile off; % Stop profiling

profile viewer; % Open the Profiler viewer to analyze results
```

Parallel Computing

FOR COMPUTATIONALLY intensive tasks, MATLAB offers parallel computing capabilities. You can take advantage of multi-core processors or distributed computing environments to speed up your code's execution. MATLAB's Parallel Computing Toolbox provides functions and tools to parallelize your code effectively.

```
% Parallel Computing Toolbox example

pool = parpool('local', 4); % Create a parallel pool with 4 workers

parfor i = 1:100

% Parallelizable task here

end

delete(pool); % Close the parallel pool when done
```

Memory Management

EFFICIENT MEMORY MANAGEMENT is crucial for code performance. MATLAB's memory usage can be optimized by releasing memory explicitly using the clear function and avoiding unnecessary data copies. Be mindful of memory-intensive operations, such as creating large temporary arrays.

```
% Memory management example

data = rand(10000, 10000); % Create a large array

result = data * 2; % Performs an operation on 'data'

clear data; % Release memory used by 'data'
```

Efficient Algorithms

SELECTING THE RIGHT algorithm for a given problem can have a significant impact on code efficiency. MATLAB provides built-in functions for various tasks, and choosing the appropriate ones can lead to faster execution times. Additionally, consider using MATLAB's optimization and solver tools for mathematical and computational problems.

```
% Using MATLAB's built-in functions and solvers

A = rand(100, 100); % Create a random matrix

b = rand(100, 1); % Create a random vector

x = A \ b; % Solve the linear system efficiently
```

Efficient MATLAB code is essential for tackling complex computational problems effectively. By following these optimization techniques and best practices, you can make your MATLAB programs faster, more reliable, and better suited for handling large-scale data and simulations.

3.2 Debugging and Error Handling

IN THIS SECTION, WE will explore the crucial aspects of debugging and error handling in MATLAB. Debugging is the process of identifying and resolving issues or "bugs" in your code, while error handling is the practice of gracefully handling unexpected errors and exceptions that may occur during program execution.

Debugging Techniques

DEBUGGING IS AN ESSENTIAL skill for any programmer. MATLAB provides several tools and techniques to help you identify and fix errors in your code:

1. The MATLAB Debugger

THE MATLAB DEBUGGER is a powerful tool that allows you to step through your code line by line, inspect variable values, and set breakpoints. You can start the debugger by clicking on the line number in the MATLAB Editor or by using the dbstop function to set breakpoints in your code.

```
% Setting breakpoints using 'dbstop'

dbstop in my_function at 20 % Sets a breakpoint at line 20 of 'my_function'
```

Once in debugging mode, you can use commands like dbstep to execute the current line and move to the next one, dbcont to continue execution until the next breakpoint, and dbquit to exit the debugger.

2. Displaying Variable Values

YOU CAN USE THE disp function or simply type variable names in the Command Window to display their current values during debugging. This helps you understand how your variables change as your code progresses.

3. Debugging Toolbar

MATLAB PROVIDES A DEBUGGING toolbar with buttons for common debugging actions, such as stepping through code, pausing execution, and inspecting variables. You can access the toolbar by clicking the "Debug" button in the MATLAB Editor.

4. Error Messages and Warnings

PAY ATTENTION TO ERROR messages and warnings that MATLAB displays in the Command Window. These messages provide valuable information about what went wrong and where the issue occurred. They often include a line number, which can help you locate the error in your code.

Error Handling

IN ADDITION TO DEBUGGING, it's essential to implement error handling mechanisms in your MATLAB code to gracefully handle unexpected situations. MATLAB provides tools like try, catch, and throw for error handling:

1. try and catch

YOU CAN USE THE try and catch blocks to surround code that may generate errors or exceptions. If an error occurs within the try block, MATLAB will execute the code inside the catch block, allowing you to handle the error.

```
try
% Code that may generate an error
result = divide_numbers(10, 0);
catch
% Handle the error gracefully
disp('An error occurred: Cannot divide by zero.');
result = NaN; % Set a default result
end
```

2. error and warning

THE error and warning functions allow you to generate custom error messages and warnings in your code. This is useful for providing informative feedback to users or for enforcing specific conditions.

```
if x < 0
error('Input must be a non-negative number.');
end
if numel(data) < 10
```

```
warning('Data size is small; results may be unreliable.');
end
```

Common Debugging Scenarios

HERE ARE SOME COMMON debugging scenarios and techniques to address them:

1. Syntax Errors

SYNTAX ERRORS OCCUR due to incorrect MATLAB syntax, such as missing parentheses or semicolons. MATLAB usually provides clear error messages with line numbers to help you locate and fix syntax errors.

2. Logical Errors

LOGICAL ERRORS ARE more challenging to identify as they do not produce error messages. They result in unexpected behavior or incorrect results in your code. To debug logical errors, use the debugging techniques mentioned earlier to inspect variable values and track the flow of your code.

3. Handling Exceptions

WHEN USING FUNCTIONS that may raise exceptions, wrap the function calls in a try-catch block to handle potential exceptions gracefully. This prevents your program from crashing due to unhandled exceptions.

```
try
% Code that may raise exceptions
```

```
result = some_function();

catch exception

% Handle the exception

disp(['An exception occurred: ', exception.message]);

end
```

Debugging and error handling are essential skills for MATLAB programmers. These techniques help you identify and resolve issues in your code, ensuring that your programs are reliable and robust. With practice and experience, you'll become more proficient at debugging and handling errors effectively.

3.3 Object-Oriented Programming in MATLAB

IN THIS SECTION, WE will explore object-oriented programming (OOP) in MATLAB. Object-oriented programming is a programming paradigm that uses objects—instances of classes—to represent and manipulate data and functionality. MATLAB supports OOP, allowing you to create and work with objects and classes. This approach can help you design more modular and maintainable code.

Classes and Objects

IN MATLAB, A CLASS is a blueprint for creating objects with specific attributes (properties) and behaviors (methods). You can define your own classes or use built-in classes provided by MATLAB. Here's a basic example of defining a class and creating objects:

```
% Define a simple class 'Person'
```

```
classdef Person

properties

FirstName

LastName

end

methods

function obj = Person(first, last)

% Constructor method

obj.FirstName = first;

obj.LastName = last;

end

function fullName = getFullName(obj)

% Method to return the full name

fullName = [obj.FirstName, ' ', obj.LastName];

end

end

end

% Create objects of the 'Person' class

person1 = Person('John', 'Doe');

person2 = Person('Jane', 'Smith');
```

```
% Access properties and call methods

fullName1 = person1.getFullName();

fullName2 = person2.getFullName();

disp(['Person 1: ', fullName1]);

disp(['Person 2: ', fullName2]);
```

In this example, we define a Person class with properties FirstName and LastName, as well as methods getFullName and a constructor obj = Person(first, last). We then create two Person objects and use their methods to access and display their full names.

Inheritance

MATLAB SUPPORTS INHERITANCE, allowing you to create new classes that inherit properties and methods from existing classes. This promotes code reuse and abstraction. Here's an example of inheritance in MATLAB:

```
% Define a base class 'Shape'

classdef Shape

properties

Color

end

methods

function obj = Shape(color)

obj.Color = color;
```

```
end
function area = computeArea(obj)
area = 0; % Placeholder for area calculation
end
end
end
% Define a derived class 'Circle' that inherits from 'Shape'
classdef Circle < Shape
properties
Radius
end
methods
function obj = Circle(color, radius)
obj@Shape(color); % Call the superclass constructor
obj.Radius = radius;
end
function area = computeArea(obj)
area = pi * obj.Radius^2;
end
end
```

```
end

% Create a 'Circle' object

circle = Circle('Red', 5);

area = circle.computeArea();

disp(['Circle area: ', num2str(area)]);
```

In this example, we define a base class Shape with a property Color and a method computeArea. We then create a derived class Circle that inherits from Shape and adds a property Radius and overrides the computeArea method. Finally, we create a Circle object and compute its area.

Encapsulation and Access Control

MATLAB SUPPORTS ACCESS control modifiers such as public, protected, and private to restrict access to properties and methods. This helps in encapsulating the implementation details and exposing only the necessary functionality to users of the class.

```
classdef MyClass

properties (Access = private)

SecretValue

end

methods

function obj = MyClass(value)

obj.SecretValue = value;

end
```

```
function result = performOperation(obj)

% Some operation using 'SecretValue'

result = obj.SecretValue * 2;

end

end

end
```

In this example, the property SecretValue is set to private access, making it inaccessible from outside the class. The performOperation method can access and manipulate SecretValue, but it cannot be accessed directly by external code.

Benefits of Object-Oriented Programming

OBJECT-ORIENTED PROGRAMMING offers several advantages in MATLAB:

- **Modularity**: OOP encourages modular code design, making it easier to manage and maintain complex systems.

- **Reusability**: You can reuse classes and objects, reducing code duplication and promoting consistency.

- **Abstraction**: OOP allows you to abstract complex data structures and operations into easily understandable and manageable objects.

- **Inheritance**: Inheritance promotes code reuse and extensibility, allowing you to build on existing code.

• **Encapsulation**: Access control and encapsulation help hide implementation details and reduce the risk of unintended interference.

Object-oriented programming in MATLAB provides a powerful way to organize and structure your code, especially for larger projects and applications. By creating well-designed classes and leveraging OOP principles, you can write cleaner, more maintainable, and efficient MATLAB code.

3.4 Graphical User Interface Development

IN THIS SECTION, WE will delve into graphical user interface (GUI) development in MATLAB. GUIs provide a visual way for users to interact with your MATLAB applications, making them user-friendly and intuitive. MATLAB offers a powerful framework for creating GUIs, enabling you to build custom interfaces for your programs.

MATLAB's GUI Development Tools

MATLAB PROVIDES TWO primary tools for creating GUIs:

1. **GUIDE (GUI Development Environment)**: GUIDE is a graphical interface within MATLAB that allows you to design and layout your GUI components visually. You can drag and drop elements like buttons, text boxes, and plots onto a canvas and specify their properties and behaviors using a user-friendly interface. GUIDE generates a corresponding .fig file and a corresponding .m file for your GUI.
2. **Programmatic GUI Development**: If you prefer a programmatic approach, you can create GUIs by writing

MATLAB code directly. You define GUI components and their properties in your code, allowing for more control and flexibility.

GUIDE-Based GUI Development

LET'S EXPLORE THE PROCESS of creating a simple GUI using GUIDE:

1. Open GUIDE by typing guide in the MATLAB Command Window.
2. In GUIDE, you can design your GUI by dragging and dropping components from the Toolbox onto the canvas. For example, you can add buttons, text fields, and axes.
3. Customize the properties of these components using the Property Inspector.
4. Define the callback functions for events like button clicks. GUIDE provides a callback editor where you can write MATLAB code to respond to user interactions.
5. Save your GUI, which generates a .fig file and a corresponding .m file that contains the GUI layout and callback functions.
6. To run your GUI, you can open the .m file and click the "Run" button in the MATLAB Editor.

Here's a basic example of a GUIDE-generated GUI:

```
% Callback function for a button in the GUI

function pushbutton1_Callback(hObject, eventdata, handles)

% Get user input from a text field

user_input = get(handles.edit1, 'String');
```

```
% Display a message based on user input

if strcmp(user_input, 'Hello')

set(handles.text2, 'String', 'Hello, MATLAB User!');

else

set(handles.text2, 'String', 'Unknown Input');

end

end
```

Programmatic GUI Development

ALTERNATIVELY, YOU can create GUIs programmatically by writing MATLAB code to define components and their properties. This method offers more control and flexibility for complex GUIs.

Here's a simplified programmatic GUI example:

```
% Create a figure window

fig = figure('Name', 'Programmatic GUI', 'Position', [100, 100, 400, 200]);

% Add a button

button = uicontrol('Style', 'pushbutton', 'String', 'Click Me', 'Position', [150, 100, 100, 30]);

% Define a callback function for the button

set(button, 'Callback', @buttonCallback);

% Callback function for the button

function buttonCallback(~, ~)
```

msgbox('Button Clicked!', 'Message', 'modal');

end

In this example, we create a figure window, add a button, and define a callback function for the button's click event.

Benefits of GUI Development in MATLAB

DEVELOPING GUIS IN MATLAB offers several advantages:

- **User-Friendly Interface**: GUIs provide an intuitive way for users to interact with your MATLAB applications, making them more accessible.
- **Data Visualization**: You can create interactive plots and graphs within your GUIs, enhancing data visualization capabilities.
- **Customization**: MATLAB's GUI development tools allow you to customize the appearance and behavior of your interfaces to meet specific requirements.
- **Integration**: You can integrate GUIs with existing MATLAB code and functions, making it easier to use and share your applications.
- **Cross-Platform Compatibility**: MATLAB GUIs are cross-platform, meaning they can be run on Windows, macOS, and Linux without modification.

Whether you choose to use GUIDE or programmatic GUI development, MATLAB's GUI capabilities empower you to create user-friendly applications with rich graphical interfaces for data analysis, simulations, and more.

3.5 Integrating MATLAB with Other Languages

IN THIS SECTION, WE will explore the integration of MATLAB with other programming languages and technologies. While MATLAB is a powerful platform for numerical computing and data analysis, there are scenarios where you may need to leverage the capabilities of other languages and tools. MATLAB offers various mechanisms for interoperability, enabling you to seamlessly work with external code and libraries.

Interoperability with C/C++

MATLAB PROVIDES THE ability to call C/C++ functions and libraries from within MATLAB code. This is accomplished using the MATLAB C/C++ Interface, which allows you to create MEX files (MATLAB executables) that bridge the gap between MATLAB and C/C++. Here's a high-level overview of the process:

1. Write your C/C++ code, including the function(s) you want to call from MATLAB.
2. Compile the C/C++ code into a MEX file using the mex command.
3. In MATLAB, you can call the compiled MEX function just like any other MATLAB function.

Example of calling a C function from MATLAB:

% C code (my_function.c)

#include "mex.h"

void mexFunction(int nlhs, mxArray *plhs[], int nrhs, const mxArray *prhs[])

```
{
// Input validation
if (nrhs != 2 || !mxIsDouble(prhs[0]) || !mxIsDouble(prhs[1])) {
mexErrMsgIdAndTxt("MyToolbox:my_function:invalidInput",
"Input must be two double matrices.");
}
// Perform some C/C++ computation
// ...
// Create output matrix
plhs[0] = mxCreateDoubleMatrix(rows, cols, mxREAL);
double *outputData = mxGetPr(plhs[0]);
// Populate the output matrix
// ...
}
```

You can then compile and use this C function within MATLAB.

Integration with Python

PYTHON IS A POPULAR programming language for a wide range of tasks, including machine learning, web development, and scientific computing. MATLAB provides a Python integration interface that allows you to execute Python code from MATLAB and exchange data between the two environments. The py module in MATLAB allows you to call Python functions and access Python libraries seamlessly.

Example of using Python within MATLAB:

```
% Execute Python code in MATLAB

output = py.example_module.example_function(42);

% Convert Python data to MATLAB data

matlabData = double(output);
```

You can also use Python libraries like NumPy and SciPy directly within MATLAB, enabling you to leverage Python's extensive ecosystem.

Java Integration

MATLAB ALSO OFFERS integration with Java, allowing you to call Java classes and methods from MATLAB code. This is particularly useful when you want to access Java libraries or utilize Java-based GUI components within your MATLAB applications.

Example of using Java within MATLAB:

```
% Create a Java object

javaObj = javaObject('java.util.ArrayList');

% Call Java methods on the object

javaObj.add('Item 1');

javaObj.add('Item 2');

% Convert Java objects to MATLAB data
```

```
matlabArray = cell(javaObj.toArray);
```

MATLAB Engine APIs

MATLAB PROVIDES ENGINE APIs for various programming languages like C/C++, Java, and .NET. These APIs allow you to embed MATLAB within applications written in those languages or call MATLAB functions from external code. This enables you to integrate MATLAB functionality into larger software projects.

Web Services and REST APIs

MATLAB ALLOWS YOU TO interact with web services and REST APIs, enabling you to exchange data and perform operations with external web resources. You can make HTTP requests, parse JSON or XML responses, and integrate MATLAB with cloud-based services and web applications.

Benefits of Integration

INTEGRATING MATLAB with other languages and technologies offers several benefits:

- **Leverage Specialized Libraries**: Access specialized libraries and tools available in other languages for specific tasks.

- **Enhance Visualization**: Combine MATLAB's data analysis capabilities with web-based visualization libraries to create interactive data dashboards and reports.

- **Scalability**: Integrate MATLAB with high-performance computing environments or cloud platforms to scale your computations and handle large datasets.

- **Cross-Platform Compatibility**: Use MATLAB alongside other languages to ensure compatibility across different platforms and environments.

- **Customization**: Build custom solutions by combining the strengths of MATLAB with other languages for specific project requirements.

By integrating MATLAB with other languages, you can extend its capabilities and address a broader range of computational and data processing challenges, making it a versatile tool for various applications.

Chapter 4: Mathematical Operations and Techniques

4.1 Matrix and Vector Operations

IN THIS SECTION, WE will explore matrix and vector operations in MATLAB. MATLAB is well-known for its powerful capabilities in linear algebra and numerical computations, making it an ideal environment for working with matrices and vectors. Whether you're solving systems of linear equations, performing eigenvalue calculations, or manipulating data in various dimensions, MATLAB provides a comprehensive set of tools for matrix and vector operations.

Basics of Matrices and Vectors

IN MATLAB, MATRICES and vectors are fundamental data structures. A matrix is a two-dimensional array, and a vector is essentially a matrix with either one row (row vector) or one column (column vector). You can create matrices and vectors using various functions and operations.

Creating Matrices and Vectors

```
% CREATING A MATRIX

A = [1, 2, 3; 4, 5, 6; 7, 8, 9];

% Creating a row vector

row_vector = [1, 2, 3];

% Creating a column vector
```

```
column_vector = [4; 5; 6];
```

Matrix and Vector Operations

MATLAB SUPPORTS A WIDE range of operations for matrices and vectors. Some of the fundamental operations include:

- **Addition and Subtraction**: You can add or subtract matrices and vectors element-wise, provided they have the same dimensions.

```
A = [1, 2; 3, 4];

B = [5, 6; 7, 8];

result = A + B; % Element-wise addition
```

- **Matrix Multiplication**: You can perform matrix multiplication using the * operator. MATLAB also provides the .* operator for element-wise multiplication.

```
A = [1, 2; 3, 4];

B = [5, 6; 7, 8];

result = A * B; % Matrix multiplication
```

- **Transpose**: The transpose of a matrix is obtained using the ' operator.

```
A = [1, 2, 3; 4, 5, 6];

A_transpose = A'; % Transpose of A
```

- **Matrix Inversion**: You can compute the inverse of a square matrix using the inv function.

```
A = [2, -1; 1, 3];
A_inverse = inv(A); % Inverse of A
```

- **Matrix Determinant**: The det function calculates the determinant of a square matrix.

```
A = [2, -1; 1, 3];
determinant = det(A); % Determinant of A
```

Solving Linear Systems

ONE OF THE MOST COMMON applications of matrix operations in MATLAB is solving systems of linear equations. You can use the \ operator or the linsolve function for this purpose.

Using the \ Operator

```
A = [2, -1; 1, 3];
b = [1; 4];
x = A \ b; % Solves the equation Ax = b for x
```

Using linsolve

```
A = [2, -1; 1, 3];
b = [1; 4];
x = linsolve(A, b); % Solves the equation Ax = b for x
```

Eigenvalue and Eigenvector Computations

MATLAB PROVIDES FUNCTIONS like eig to compute eigenvalues and eigenvectors of a matrix.

```
A = [4, -2; 1, 1];

[eigenvalues, eigenvectors] = eig(A);
```

Singular Value Decomposition (SVD)

THE svd function allows you to perform singular value decomposition of a matrix.

```
A = [1, 2; 3, 4; 5, 6];

[U, S, V] = svd(A);
```

These are just some of the basic operations and techniques for working with matrices and vectors in MATLAB. MATLAB's extensive linear algebra capabilities make it a powerful tool for various applications in engineering, science, and data analysis. In the subsequent sections of this chapter, we will delve deeper into specific applications of matrix and vector operations in fields such as linear algebra applications, differential equations, signal processing, and optimization techniques.

4.2 Linear Algebra Applications

IN THIS SECTION, WE will explore the applications of linear algebra in MATLAB. Linear algebra plays a fundamental role in many scientific and engineering disciplines, and MATLAB provides a rich set of tools for solving linear algebraic problems efficiently.

Solving Systems of Linear Equations

ONE OF THE PRIMARY applications of linear algebra in MATLAB is solving systems of linear equations. These equations can be represented in matrix form as **Ax** = **b**, where **A** is a coefficient matrix, **x** is the vector of unknowns, and **b** is the right-hand side vector. MATLAB provides several methods for solving such systems, including direct methods like Gaussian elimination and iterative methods like conjugate gradient descent.

Direct Methods

MATLAB'S BACKSLASH operator \ and the linsolve function are commonly used for solving linear systems using direct methods. For example:

```
A = [2, -1; 1, 3];

b = [1; 4];

x = A \ b; % Solves the equation Ax = b for x
```

Iterative Methods

IF YOU ARE DEALING with large, sparse, or ill-conditioned systems, iterative methods may be more suitable. MATLAB provides functions like pcg (Preconditioned Conjugate Gradient) for solving linear systems iteratively.

```
A = gallery('poisson', 4);

b = ones(16, 1);

x0 = zeros(16, 1);
```

```
[x, flag, relres] = pcg(A, b, 1e-6, 100, [], [], x0); % Solve Ax = b iteratively
```

Eigenvalue Problems

EIGENVALUE PROBLEMS are prevalent in various fields, including structural engineering, quantum mechanics, and data analysis. MATLAB's eig function can be used to compute eigenvalues and eigenvectors of a matrix.

```
A = [4, -2; 1, 1];

[eigenvalues, eigenvectors] = eig(A);
```

Singular Value Decomposition (SVD)

SINGULAR VALUE DECOMPOSITION (SVD) is a powerful tool in linear algebra with applications in dimensionality reduction, image compression, and data analysis. MATLAB's svd function allows you to perform SVD on a matrix.

```
A = [1, 2; 3, 4; 5, 6];

[U, S, V] = svd(A);
```

Linear Transformations and Geometry

LINEAR ALGEBRA IS USED extensively in computer graphics and computer vision. MATLAB can represent and apply linear transformations using matrices. For example, you can perform translations, rotations, and scaling of 2D and 3D objects using matrix operations.

```
% Translation matrix

translation_matrix = [1, 0, dx; 0, 1, dy; 0, 0, 1];
```

```
% Rotation matrix (2D)

theta = pi/4; % 45 degrees

rotation_matrix = [cos(theta), -sin(theta), 0; sin(theta), cos(theta), 0; 0, 0, 1];

% Scaling matrix (2D)

scaling_matrix = [sx, 0, 0; 0, sy, 0; 0, 0, 1];

% Apply transformations to a point (homogeneous coordinates)

point = [x; y; 1];

transformed_point = translation_matrix * rotation_matrix * scaling_matrix * point;
```

Applications in Machine Learning

LINEAR ALGEBRA FORMS the foundation of many machine learning algorithms, especially those involving matrix operations like linear regression, principal component analysis (PCA), and support vector machines (SVM). MATLAB's built-in functions and libraries make it a convenient platform for implementing and experimenting with these algorithms.

```
% Linear regression example

X = [1, 1; 2, 1; 3, 1; 4, 1];

y = [2; 4; 6; 8];

coefficients = X \ y; % Linear regression coefficients
```

These are just a few examples of how linear algebra is applied in MATLAB across various domains. MATLAB's efficiency in handling matrix operations and its wide range of built-in functions make it a valuable tool for researchers, engineers, and scientists dealing with linear algebraic problems. In the subsequent sections of this chapter, we will explore more advanced topics, such as differential equations, Fourier transforms, and optimization techniques, all of which build upon the foundational concepts of linear algebra.

4.3 Differential Equations and Integration

DIFFERENTIAL EQUATIONS are fundamental in describing dynamic systems and phenomena in various fields, including physics, engineering, biology, and economics. MATLAB provides comprehensive tools for solving ordinary differential equations (ODEs) and partial differential equations (PDEs), making it a powerful environment for modeling and simulating dynamic systems.

Solving Ordinary Differential Equations (ODEs)

ODES DESCRIBE HOW A system changes over time. MATLAB offers several functions to solve ODEs numerically, including the ode45, ode23, and ode15s solvers. These solvers are capable of handling a wide range of ODEs, from simple first-order equations to complex systems of coupled ODEs.

Example of a First-Order ODE

*% DEFINE THE ODE: DY/dx = -2*y*

ode = @(x, y) -2*y;

% Define the initial condition: y(0) = 1

```
initial_condition = 1;

% Define the time span

tspan = [0, 5];

% Solve the ODE using ode45

[t, y] = ode45(ode, tspan, initial_condition);

% Plot the solution

plot(t, y);

xlabel('Time');

ylabel('y(t)');

title('Solution of dy/dx = -2*y');
```

Example of a Second-Order ODE

```
% DEFINE THE ODE: D^2y/dx^2 + 2*dy/dx + 2*y = 0

ode = @(x, y) [y(2); -2*y(2) - 2*y(1)];

% Define the initial conditions: y(0) = 1, dy/dx(0) = 0

initial_conditions = [1; 0];

% Solve the ODE using ode45

tspan = [0, 10];

[t, y] = ode45(ode, tspan, initial_conditions);

% Plot the solution

plot(t, y(:, 1));
```

```
xlabel('Time');

ylabel('y(t)');

title('Solution of d^2y/dx^2 + 2*dy/dx + 2*y = 0');
```

Solving Partial Differential Equations (PDEs)

PDES DESCRIBE HOW A system changes over multiple independent variables, such as time and space. MATLAB provides tools for solving a wide range of PDEs, including elliptic, parabolic, and hyperbolic equations, using finite difference, finite element, and finite volume methods. The pdepe solver is commonly used for solving time-dependent PDEs.

Example of Solving a Time-Dependent PDE

```
% DEFINE THE PDE: ∂U/∂t = ∂^2u/∂x^2

pde = @(x, t, u, dudx) dudx - 2;

% Define the spatial domain (0 <= x <= 1) and time span (0 <= t <= 1)

xmesh = linspace(0, 1, 100);

tspan = linspace(0, 1, 50);

% Define the initial condition: u(x, 0) = sin(pi*x)

initial_condition = sin(pi*xmesh);

% Solve the PDE using pdepe

sol = pdepe(0, pde, initial_condition, [], xmesh, tspan);

% Create a surface plot of the solution
```

```
[X, T] = meshgrid(xmesh, tspan);

surf(X, T, sol');

xlabel('Spatial Domain (x)');

ylabel('Time (t)');

zlabel('u(x, t)');

title('Solution of ∂u/∂t = ∂^2u/∂x^2');
```

Integration Techniques

IN ADDITION TO SOLVING differential equations, MATLAB provides tools for numerical integration, which is essential for evaluating definite integrals and performing numerical analysis.

Example of Numerical Integration

```
% DEFINE THE FUNCTION to be integrated: f(x) = sin(x)

fun = @(x) sin(x);

% Define the integration limits: [0, pi]

a = 0;

b = pi;

% Perform numerical integration using the quad function

integral_value = quad(fun, a, b);

fprintf('The integral of sin(x) from 0 to pi is approximately %.4f\n', integral_value);
```

MATLAB also supports adaptive quadrature, which can handle a wide range of functions, including those with singularities and oscillatory behavior.

These capabilities make MATLAB a versatile environment for solving differential equations and performing numerical integration, allowing engineers, scientists, and researchers to model and simulate complex dynamic systems and perform various mathematical analyses.

4.4 Fourier Transforms and Signal Processing

IN THIS SECTION, WE will explore the use of MATLAB for Fourier transforms and signal processing. Fourier analysis is a fundamental mathematical tool used to decompose complex signals into their constituent frequencies. MATLAB provides a comprehensive set of functions for performing Fourier analysis and signal processing tasks, making it an essential tool for engineers, scientists, and researchers working with data from various domains.

Discrete Fourier Transform (DFT)

THE DISCRETE FOURIER Transform (DFT) is a mathematical transformation used to convert a discrete-time signal into its frequency domain representation. MATLAB provides the fft function to compute the DFT efficiently. Here's a basic example:

```
% Generate a sample signal: a sum of two sine waves

Fs = 1000; % Sampling frequency (Hz)

t = 0:1/Fs:1; % Time vector

f1 = 5; % Frequency of the first sine wave (Hz)
```

```
f2 = 20; % Frequency of the second sine wave (Hz)

signal = sin(2*pi*f1*t) + sin(2*pi*f2*t);

% Compute the DFT

N = length(signal); % Number of samples

frequencies = Fs*(0:(N/2))/N; % Frequency axis

signal_fft = fft(signal);

magnitude_spectrum = abs(signal_fft/N);
```

The signal_fft variable contains the complex-valued DFT coefficients, and magnitude_spectrum represents the magnitude of the frequencies in the signal.

Inverse Fourier Transform

TO TRANSFORM THE FREQUENCY domain representation back to the time domain, you can use the Inverse Discrete Fourier Transform (IDFT) implemented in MATLAB as ifft. Here's an example:

```
% Compute the inverse DFT

reconstructed_signal = ifft(signal_fft);
```

The reconstructed_signal variable contains the time-domain signal reconstructed from the frequency domain representation.

Spectrogram and Short-Time Fourier Transform (STFT)

THE SPECTROGRAM IS a valuable tool for analyzing time-varying signals. MATLAB's spectrogram function computes the Short-Time Fourier Transform (STFT) of a signal and provides a visual representation of its frequency content over time. Here's an example:

```
% Compute the spectrogram

window_length = 128; % Length of the analysis window

overlap = 64; % Overlap between successive windows

nfft = 256; % Number of FFT points

[s, f, t] = spectrogram(signal, window_length, overlap, nfft, Fs);

% Plot the spectrogram

imagesc(t, f, 10*log10(abs(s)));

axis xy;

xlabel('Time (s)');

ylabel('Frequency (Hz)');

title('Spectrogram of the Signal');
```

The spectrogram function returns the spectrogram s, the frequency axis f, and the time axis t.

Filtering and Signal Processing

MATLAB OFFERS VARIOUS functions for filtering and processing signals, including low-pass, high-pass, band-pass, and band-stop filters. The filter function allows you to apply digital filters to signals. Here's a simple example of a low-pass filter:

```
% Design a low-pass filter
```

```
cutoff_frequency = 50; % Cutoff frequency (Hz)

filter_order = 4; % Filter order

[b, a] = butter(filter_order, cutoff_frequency/(Fs/2), 'low');

% Apply the filter to the signal

filtered_signal = filter(b, a, signal);
```

Fast Fourier Transform (FFT) for Efficiency

WHEN DEALING WITH LARGE datasets or real-time signal processing, MATLAB's Fast Fourier Transform (FFT) functions (fft and ifft) provide significant computational advantages. They efficiently compute the DFT and IDFT, respectively, especially for signals with a power of two lengths.

```
% Compute the FFT and IFFT

signal_fft = fft(signal, N); % N is a power of two for efficiency

reconstructed_signal = ifft(signal_fft, N);
```

These are just a few examples of how MATLAB is used for Fourier transforms and signal processing. MATLAB's extensive signal processing toolbox offers numerous functions for filtering, windowing, spectral analysis, and more, making it a powerful platform for analyzing and manipulating signals from various sources, including audio, biomedical data, and sensor measurements.

4.5 Optimization Techniques

OPTIMIZATION IS A CRUCIAL aspect of mathematical modeling and problem-solving in engineering, science, and various other fields. MATLAB provides a comprehensive set of tools for solving optimization problems, from linear programming to nonlinear optimization and mixed-integer programming. In this section, we will explore some of the optimization techniques available in MATLAB and how they can be applied to real-world problems.

Linear Programming (LP)

LINEAR PROGRAMMING is a mathematical technique used to find the optimal solution to a linear objective function subject to linear constraints. MATLAB's Optimization Toolbox offers the linprog function for solving linear programming problems. Here's a simple example:

```
% Define the objective function coefficients

c = [2; 3];

% Define the inequality constraints: A*x <= b

A = [-1, 1; 1, 2];

b = [1; 4];

% Define the lower and upper bounds on variables: lb <= x <= ub

lb = zeros(2, 1); % x >= 0

ub = []; % No upper bounds

% Solve the linear programming problem

[x, fval, exitflag] = linprog(c, [], [], A, b, lb, ub);

% Display the results

disp('Optimal solution:');
```

```
disp(x);

disp(['Optimal objective function value: ', num2str(fval)]);

disp(['Exit flag: ', num2str(exitflag)]);
```

The linprog function finds the values of variables that maximize or minimize the linear objective function while satisfying the linear inequality constraints.

Nonlinear Optimization

NONLINEAR OPTIMIZATION problems involve nonlinear objective functions and constraints. MATLAB's Optimization Toolbox provides various functions for solving nonlinear optimization problems, including fminunc, fmincon, and lsqnonlin. Here's an example using fminunc to minimize a nonlinear function:

```
% Define the objective function to be minimized

fun = @(x) x(1)^2 + x(2)^2;

% Define an initial guess

x0 = [1; 1];

% Minimize the objective function using fminunc

options = optimoptions('fminunc', 'Display', 'iter');

[x, fval] = fminunc(fun, x0, options);

% Display the results

disp('Optimal solution:');

disp(x);
```

```
disp(['Optimal objective function value: ', num2str(fval)]);
```

In this example, fminunc finds the values of variables that minimize the nonlinear objective function.

Global Optimization

GLOBAL OPTIMIZATION problems involve finding the global minimum or maximum of a function, which can be challenging due to multiple local minima/maxima. MATLAB's Optimization Toolbox offers the globaloptim function, which provides a framework for global optimization using various algorithms. Here's a basic example:

```
% Define the objective function to be minimized

fun = @(x) x(1)^4 - 2*x(1)^2 + x(2)^2 + x(1)*x(2) - x(2);

% Define variable bounds

lb = [-5; -5];

ub = [5; 5];

% Perform global optimization using the 'fmincon' solver

opts = optimoptions('fmincon', 'Display', 'off');

problem = createOptimProblem('fmincon', 'x0', [0; 0], 'objective', fun, 'lb', lb, 'ub', ub, 'options', opts);

ms = MultiStart('Display', 'off');

[x, fval] = run(ms, problem, 10);

% Display the results

disp('Optimal solution:');
```

```
disp(x);

disp(['Optimal objective function value: ', num2str(fval)]);
```

The MultiStart approach repeatedly applies a local optimization solver to random starting points and returns the best solution found.

Mixed-Integer Linear Programming (MILP) and Mixed-Integer Nonlinear Programming (MINLP)

WHEN OPTIMIZATION PROBLEMS involve both continuous and discrete variables, MATLAB supports Mixed-Integer Linear Programming (MILP) and Mixed-Integer Nonlinear Programming (MINLP) using the intlinprog and fmincon functions with appropriate constraints on integer variables.

```
% Define the MILP objective function and constraints

intcon = [1, 2]; % Integer variables

f = [1; 2]; % Coefficients of the objective function

A = [-1, 1; 1, 2];

b = [1; 4];

lb = [0; 0];

ub = [1; 1];

% Solve the MILP problem

[x, fval] = intlinprog(f, intcon, A, b, [], [], lb, ub);

% Display the results

disp('Optimal solution:');
```

```
disp(x);

disp(['Optimal objective function value: ', num2str(fval)]);
```

In this example, we define integer variables and constraints to solve a MILP problem.

These are just a few examples of the optimization techniques available in MATLAB. MATLAB's optimization capabilities are widely used in fields such as operations research, engineering design, finance, and data science, where finding the best solution to complex problems is crucial. Researchers and practitioners can leverage MATLAB's optimization tools to efficiently tackle a wide range of optimization problems.

Chapter 5: Data Analysis and Visualization

5.1 Importing and Exporting Data

IN THIS SECTION, WE will explore how MATLAB facilitates the importing and exporting of data from various file formats. MATLAB provides a range of functions and tools to handle data files, making it a powerful environment for data analysis and visualization.

Importing Data

MATLAB OFFERS SEVERAL methods to import data from external sources, including text files, spreadsheets, and databases. The readtable and readmatrix functions are commonly used to read data from text files and spreadsheets.

Importing Data from a Text File

```
% SPECIFY THE PATH TO the text file

filename = 'data.txt';

% Use readtable to import data from the text file

data = readtable(filename);

% Display the imported data

disp(data);
```

Importing Data from an Excel Spreadsheet

```
% SPECIFY THE PATH TO the Excel file

filename = 'data.xlsx';

% Use readtable to import data from the Excel file

data = readtable(filename);

% Display the imported data

disp(data);
```

Exporting Data

AFTER PERFORMING DATA analysis or processing in MATLAB, you can export the results to various file formats, including text files, spreadsheets, and more. The writetable and writematrix functions are commonly used for exporting data.

Exporting Data to a Text File

```
% CREATE A SAMPLE DATA table

data = table([1; 2; 3], [4; 5; 6], 'VariableNames', {'Column1', 'Column2'});

% Specify the file name for export

filename = 'exported_data.txt';

% Use writetable to export data to a text file

writetable(data, filename, 'Delimiter', '\t'); % Tab-delimited
```

Exporting Data to an Excel Spreadsheet

```
% CREATE A SAMPLE DATA matrix

data = [1, 2, 3; 4, 5, 6];

% Specify the file name for export

filename = 'exported_data.xlsx';

% Use writematrix to export data to an Excel file

writematrix(data, filename, 'Sheet', 'Sheet1');
```

Data Exploration and Preprocessing

BEFORE PERFORMING IN-depth data analysis and visualization, it's often necessary to explore and preprocess the data. MATLAB provides various functions for data exploration, including summary statistics, missing data handling, and data visualization. Here's a basic example of generating summary statistics for a dataset:

```
% Load a sample dataset

load('fisheriris.mat');

% Calculate summary statistics

summary(irisdata);
```

Data Visualization

ONCE DATA IS IMPORTED and preprocessed, MATLAB offers a wide range of data visualization tools to help you understand and present your data effectively. The plot, scatter, histogram, and boxplot functions are commonly used for data visualization. Here's a simple example of creating a scatter plot:

```
% Create a scatter plot of sepal length vs. sepal width

scatter(irisdata(:, 1), irisdata(:, 2));

xlabel('Sepal Length (cm)');

ylabel('Sepal Width (cm)');

title('Scatter Plot of Sepal Length vs. Sepal Width');
```

These are just a few examples of how MATLAB simplifies the process of importing, exploring, and visualizing data. Whether you're working with small datasets or large datasets, MATLAB's data handling capabilities streamline the workflow, making it a valuable tool for data analysts and scientists. In the subsequent sections of this chapter, we will delve deeper into statistical analysis, advanced visualization techniques, and more, building upon the foundational skills discussed here.

5.2 Data Cleaning and Preprocessing

IN THIS SECTION, WE will explore the crucial steps of data cleaning and preprocessing in MATLAB. These steps are essential for preparing data for analysis and visualization, as real-world data often contains errors, missing values, and inconsistencies that can affect the quality and reliability of your results.

Handling Missing Data

DEALING WITH MISSING data is a common challenge in data analysis. MATLAB provides various techniques for handling missing values, such as removing rows or columns with missing data, imputing missing values, or interpolating to fill in gaps.

Removing Rows or Columns with Missing Data

```
% LOAD A SAMPLE DATASET with missing values

load('sampledata.mat');

% Remove rows with missing data

cleaned_data = rmmissing(data);

% Remove columns with missing data

cleaned_data = rmmissing(data, 'DataVariables', {'Column1', 'Column2'});
```

Imputing Missing Values

```
% LOAD A SAMPLE DATASET with missing values

load('sampledata.mat');

% Impute missing values with the mean of the column

data_mean_imputed = fillmissing(data, 'mean');
```

Data Transformation

DATA TRANSFORMATION techniques are used to prepare data for analysis by modifying its distribution, scaling, or structure. Common transformations include normalization, standardization, and log transformation.

Normalization

NORMALIZATION SCALES data to have a mean of 0 and a standard deviation of 1, bringing all variables to a common scale.

% Load a dataset to normalize

load('normalizedata.mat');

% Normalize the data

normalized_data = normalize(data);

Standardization

STANDARDIZATION SCALES data to have a mean of 0 and a standard deviation of 1, but unlike normalization, it does not bound data between specific values.

% Load a dataset to standardize

load('standardizedata.mat');

% Standardize the data

standardized_data = zscore(data);

Data Aggregation and Resampling

DEPENDING ON THE ANALYSIS goals, you may need to aggregate data or resample it to a different time interval. MATLAB provides functions to perform these operations.

Data Aggregation

% LOAD A DATASET FOR aggregation

load('aggregatedata.mat');

% Aggregate data by calculating the mean for each day

daily_mean_data = retime(data, 'daily', 'mean');

Data Resampling

% LOAD A DATASET FOR resampling

load('resampledata.mat');

% Resample data to a higher frequency using interpolation

resampled_data = resample(data, 1, 10);

Handling Categorical Data

CATEGORICAL DATA IS data that represents categories or labels rather than numerical values. MATLAB provides functions to convert categorical data to numerical format for analysis.

% Create a categorical array

categories = {'Category A', 'Category B', 'Category C'};

categorical_data = categorical(categories, categories);

% Convert categorical data to numerical using one-hot encoding

numerical_data = dummyvar(categorical_data);

Data Validation

VALIDATING DATA IS crucial to ensure its accuracy and consistency. MATLAB offers tools to perform data validation, including checks for outliers, anomalies, and consistency.

% Load a dataset for outlier detection

load('outlierdata.mat');

% Detect outliers using the Z-score method

```
z_scores = zscore(data);

outliers = abs(z_scores) > 3;

% Remove outliers from the dataset

cleaned_data = data(~outliers, :);
```

These data cleaning and preprocessing techniques are fundamental to ensuring that your data is in a suitable state for analysis and visualization. Depending on the specific characteristics and quality of your data, you may need to apply one or more of these techniques to achieve accurate and reliable results in your data-driven projects. MATLAB's extensive set of functions and tools simplifies these tasks, allowing you to focus on the analysis and insights derived from your data.

5.3 Statistical Analysis with MATLAB

STATISTICAL ANALYSIS is a fundamental component of data analysis, allowing you to uncover patterns, relationships, and insights within your data. In this section, we will explore how MATLAB provides a comprehensive set of tools for performing various statistical analyses.

Descriptive Statistics

DESCRIPTIVE STATISTICS summarize and describe the main features of a dataset. MATLAB offers functions to calculate common descriptive statistics, such as mean, median, standard deviation, variance, and quartiles.

```
% Load a dataset for descriptive statistics

load('descriptivestatsdata.mat');
```

```
% Calculate mean and standard deviation

mean_data = mean(data);

std_data = std(data);

% Calculate median and quartiles

median_data = median(data);

quartiles_data = quantile(data, [0.25, 0.75]);
```

Hypothesis Testing

HYPOTHESIS TESTING is used to make inferences about population parameters based on sample data. MATLAB provides functions for conducting various hypothesis tests, including t-tests, ANOVA, chi-square tests, and more.

```
% Load datasets for hypothesis testing

load('hypothesistestdata.mat');

% Perform a t-test to compare two sample means

[h, p, ci, stats] = ttest2(sample1, sample2);

% Perform one-way ANOVA to compare multiple groups

[p, tbl, stats] = anova1(data, group_labels);
```

Regression Analysis

REGRESSION ANALYSIS explores the relationship between one or more independent variables and a dependent variable. MATLAB supports various regression techniques, including linear regression, logistic regression, and polynomial regression.

```
% Load data for linear regression

load('linearregressiondata.mat');

% Fit a linear regression model

mdl = fitlm(x, y);

% Display the regression coefficients and statistics

disp(mdl.Coefficients.Estimate);

disp(mdl.Rsquared.Ordinary);
```

Time Series Analysis

TIME SERIES DATA ANALYSIS is crucial for understanding and forecasting temporal data. MATLAB provides functions for time series modeling, including autoregressive integrated moving average (ARIMA) modeling and seasonal decomposition.

```
% Load a time series dataset

load('timeseriesdata.mat');

% Perform seasonal decomposition

decomposition = seasonaldecompose(data);

% Fit an ARIMA model

mdl = arima(data);
```

Data Distributions and Probability

MATLAB ALLOWS YOU TO work with various probability distributions and perform probability calculations. You can generate random numbers from distributions, calculate probability density functions, cumulative distribution functions, and more.

```
% Generate random numbers from a normal distribution

mu = 0;

sigma = 1;

random_data = normrnd(mu, sigma, 1000, 1);

% Calculate probability density function

pdf_values = normpdf(random_data, mu, sigma);

% Calculate cumulative distribution function

cdf_values = normcdf(random_data, mu, sigma);
```

Multivariate Analysis

MULTIVARIATE ANALYSIS techniques help analyze datasets with multiple variables. MATLAB offers tools for principal component analysis (PCA), factor analysis, and cluster analysis.

```
% Load a multivariate dataset

load('multivariatedata.mat');

% Perform principal component analysis (PCA)

[coeff, score, latent, tsquared, explained] = pca(data);

% Perform hierarchical cluster analysis

tree = linkage(data, 'ward');

dendrogram(tree);
```

These examples demonstrate the diverse set of statistical analysis techniques available in MATLAB. Whether you need to perform basic descriptive statistics, conduct hypothesis tests, build regression models, analyze time series data, work with probability distributions, or explore multivariate relationships, MATLAB provides the tools to support your statistical analysis needs. These capabilities are invaluable for researchers, data scientists, and analysts working with data from various domains.

5.4 Creating Plots and Graphs

DATA VISUALIZATION is a crucial aspect of data analysis, as it helps you gain insights from your data and communicate your findings effectively. MATLAB offers a wide range of tools and functions for creating various types of plots and graphs, allowing you to visualize data in meaningful ways.

Basic Plotting

THE MOST FUNDAMENTAL plot in MATLAB is the line plot, which is created using the plot function. You can visualize relationships between two variables by plotting data points and connecting them with lines.

```
% Create a simple line plot

x = linspace(0, 2*pi, 100);

y = sin(x);

% Plot the sine wave

plot(x, y);

xlabel('Angle (radians)');
```

```
ylabel('Sin(x)');

title('Sine Wave');
```

Scatter Plots

SCATTER PLOTS ARE USEFUL for visualizing the distribution of data points in two dimensions. MATLAB's scatter function allows you to create scatter plots easily.

```
% Create a scatter plot of random data

x = rand(100, 1);

y = rand(100, 1);

% Plot the scatter plot

scatter(x, y);

xlabel('X-axis');

ylabel('Y-axis');

title('Random Scatter Plot');
```

Bar Charts

BAR CHARTS ARE EFFECTIVE for visualizing categorical data or comparing different categories. You can use the bar function to create bar charts.

```
% Create a bar chart of sales data

categories = {'Category A', 'Category B', 'Category C'};

sales = [1200, 800, 1500];
```

```
% Plot the bar chart

bar(categories, sales);

xlabel('Categories');

ylabel('Sales (USD)');

title('Sales by Category');
```

Histograms

HISTOGRAMS HELP YOU visualize the distribution of a continuous variable. MATLAB's histogram function allows you to create histograms and customize bin sizes.

```
% Create a histogram of exam scores

scores = [75, 85, 90, 78, 92, 88, 68, 72, 94, 82, 76, 89, 71];

histogram(scores, 'BinWidth', 5);

xlabel('Score Range');

ylabel('Frequency');

title('Exam Score Distribution');
```

Box Plots

BOX PLOTS PROVIDE A summary of the distribution of a dataset, including median, quartiles, and outliers. MATLAB's boxplot function is used for creating box plots.

```
% Create a box plot of temperature data

temperatures = [25, 30, 22, 18, 28, 32, 27, 33, 29, 23];
```

```
boxplot(temperatures);

ylabel('Temperature (°C)');

title('Temperature Box Plot');
```

3D Plots

FOR VISUALIZING DATA in three dimensions, MATLAB provides functions like plot3, scatter3, and surf for creating 3D line plots, scatter plots, and surface plots.

```
% Create a 3D scatter plot

x = rand(100, 1);

y = rand(100, 1);

z = rand(100, 1);

scatter3(x, y, z, 'filled');

xlabel('X-axis');

ylabel('Y-axis');

zlabel('Z-axis');

title('3D Scatter Plot');
```

Customizing Plots

MATLAB ALLOWS EXTENSIVE customization of plots. You can change line colors, markers, axis labels, legends, and more to enhance the visual appeal and clarity of your plots.

```
% Customizing a plot
```

```
x = linspace(0, 2*pi, 100);

y1 = sin(x);

y2 = cos(x);

plot(x, y1, 'r-', 'LineWidth', 2); % Red solid line

hold on; % Keep the current axes

plot(x, y2, 'b—', 'LineWidth', 1.5); % Blue dashed line

xlabel('Angle (radians)');

ylabel('Function Value');

title('Customized Plot');

legend('sin(x)', 'cos(x)');

grid on; % Display grid lines
```

These are just a few examples of the types of plots you can create using MATLAB. Whether you need to visualize simple data relationships or complex multidimensional data, MATLAB's extensive plotting capabilities allow you to present your data in a clear and informative manner. Data visualization is a critical step in the data analysis process, enabling you to discover patterns, trends, and anomalies in your data.

5.5 Advanced Visualization Techniques

IN ADDITION TO THE basic plotting techniques mentioned in the previous section, MATLAB offers advanced visualization capabilities to handle more complex and specialized data visualization requirements. These advanced techniques allow you to create intricate and informative visualizations for various domains and data types.

Geographic Data Visualization

FOR VISUALIZING GEOGRAPHIC data, MATLAB provides mapping and geospatial tools. You can create maps, plot data on maps, and perform geospatial analysis. The Mapping Toolbox offers functions for displaying geographical data, generating contour plots, and working with shapefiles.

```
% Create a basic map with coastlines

figure;

worldmap;

% Plot data on the map (e.g., earthquake locations)

load coastlines;

load earthquakes;

scatterm(earthquakes.Latitude, earthquakes.Longitude, 10,
earthquakes.Depth, 'filled');

title('Earthquake Locations and Depths');

colorbar;
```

3D Visualization

MATLAB EXCELS IN 3D visualization, allowing you to create 3D plots, surface plots, and volumetric visualizations. These techniques are essential for visualizing complex 3D data, such as 3D point clouds, medical images, and simulations.

```
% Create a 3D surface plot

[X, Y] = meshgrid(-2:0.1:2);

Z = X.^2 + Y.^2;

figure;

surf(X, Y, Z);

xlabel('X-axis');

ylabel('Y-axis');

zlabel('Z-axis');

title('3D Surface Plot');
```

Interactive Plotting with App Designer

IF YOU NEED TO CREATE interactive plots and applications, MATLAB's App Designer allows you to build custom user interfaces with interactive components like sliders, buttons, and plots. This is particularly useful for creating interactive dashboards and data exploration tools.

```
% Create an interactive plot using App Designer

% (Code generated by App Designer)

% Launch the App Designer GUI

appdesigner;
```

Animation

FOR VISUALIZING DYNAMIC processes or time-dependent data, MATLAB supports animation. You can create animations to visualize how data changes over time, simulating scenarios, or demonstrating complex concepts.

```
% Create a simple animation of a moving sine wave

t = linspace(0, 2*pi, 100);

for i = 1:100

y = sin(t + i/10);

plot(t, y);

xlim([0, 2*pi]);

ylim([-1, 1]);

pause(0.1); % Pause to control animation speed

end
```

Custom Plot Interactions

MATLAB ALLOWS YOU TO create custom interactions with plots. You can add callbacks to respond to user interactions, such as mouse clicks or key presses, to enhance the user experience.

```
% Create a plot with a custom callback function

x = linspace(0, 2*pi, 100);

y = sin(x);

figure;

plot(x, y);

xlabel('Angle (radians)');
```

```
ylabel('Sin(x)');

title('Custom Plot Interaction');

% Add a callback function for mouse clicks

set(gcf, 'ButtonDownFcn', @(src, event) customCallback(src, event,
x, y));
```

Specialized Visualization Toolboxes

MATLAB OFFERS SPECIALIZED toolboxes for various domains, such as image processing, signal processing, and bioinformatics. These toolboxes provide functions and capabilities tailored to specific data types and analysis needs.

```
% Example of using the Image Processing Toolbox

% (Code for illustrative purposes)

% Read and display an image

image = imread('example.jpg');

imshow(image);

% Perform image processing operations

filtered_image = imfilter(image, fspecial('gaussian', [5 5], 2));

imshow(filtered_image);

title('Image Processing Example');
```

These advanced visualization techniques empower you to create sophisticated visualizations that cater to the specific demands of your data and domain. Whether you need to visualize geographic data, work in 3D, build interactive applications, create animations, enable custom plot interactions, or leverage specialized toolboxes, MATLAB provides a versatile and powerful platform for advanced data visualization.

Chapter 6: Simulink: An Introduction 6.1. Overview of Simulink 6.2. Simulink vs. MATLAB: Understanding the Differences 6.3. Basic Simulink Models 6.4. Simulating Dynamic Systems 6.5. Simulink for Control Systems

---

Chapter 6: Simulink: An Introduction

6.1. Overview of Simulink

SIMULINK IS A POWERFUL visual programming environment in MATLAB that is widely used for modeling, simulating, and analyzing dynamic systems. It provides a graphical user interface (GUI) for designing and simulating complex systems, making it particularly well-suited for control systems, signal processing, and multidomain simulation. In this section, we will provide an overview of Simulink, its key features, and how it integrates with MATLAB.

Simulink Basics

AT ITS CORE, SIMULINK allows you to represent dynamic systems as block diagrams. Each block represents a specific mathematical or logical operation, and you connect these blocks to define the system's behavior. Simulink provides a vast library of predefined blocks for various domains, including mathematics, control systems, signal processing, and more.

```
% Example of a simple Simulink model

open_system('simulink/demo_sldemo_absbrake');
```

Block Diagram Modeling

BLOCK DIAGRAM MODELING in Simulink simplifies the representation of complex systems. You can easily create models by dragging and dropping blocks onto the canvas, connecting them, and specifying parameters. This visual approach makes it accessible to engineers and scientists without extensive programming knowledge.

```
% Create a simple Simulink model programmatically

model = 'simple_motor_model';

open_system(new_system(model));

add_block('simulink/Sources/Step', [model '/Step Input']);

add_block('simulink/Continuous/Transfer Fcn', [model '/Motor']);

add_line(model, 'Step Input/1', 'Motor/1');

set_param([model '/Step Input'], 'Time', '0:0.01:5');

set_param([model '/Motor'], 'Numerator', '1', 'Denominator', '[1 2]');
```

Simulation and Analysis

SIMULINK ALLOWS YOU to simulate the behavior of your models over time. You can define input signals, set simulation parameters, and run simulations to observe the system's response. Simulink provides various tools for analyzing simulation results, including time-domain and frequency-domain analysis.

```
% Simulate a Simulink model

simOut = sim('simple_motor_model');

plot(simOut.get('tout'), simOut.get('yout'));

xlabel('Time');

ylabel('Response');

title('Simulink Simulation Results');
```

MATLAB Integration

ONE OF THE STRENGTHS of Simulink is its tight integration with MATLAB. You can use MATLAB scripts and functions within Simulink models, allowing for complex data processing, control algorithms, and custom analysis. This integration enables seamless interaction between the two environments.

```
% Use MATLAB script in a Simulink model

open_system('simulink/demo_sldemo_howto_export');
```

Targeting Hardware

SIMULINK SUPPORTS HARDWARE-in-the-loop (HIL) and real-time simulation, allowing you to interface with physical hardware for testing and validation. This capability is essential for developing and verifying control systems and embedded applications.

```
% Real-time simulation with Simulink

open_system('simulink/demo_sldemo_rti');
```

Application Areas

SIMULINK FINDS APPLICATIONS in a wide range of industries and domains, including aerospace, automotive, robotics, communications, and more. It is a valuable tool for developing and testing control systems, signal processing algorithms, and multidomain simulations.

In summary, Simulink is a versatile and powerful tool for modeling and simulating dynamic systems. Its graphical interface simplifies the representation of complex systems, and its tight integration with MATLAB enables seamless data processing and analysis. Whether you are working on control systems, signal processing, or multidomain simulations, Simulink is an invaluable resource for engineers and scientists.

6.2. Simulink vs. MATLAB: Understanding the Differences

SIMULINK AND MATLAB are both powerful tools offered by MathWorks, but they serve different purposes and are used in distinct ways. In this section, we will explore the key differences between Simulink and MATLAB to help you understand their respective roles in the world of computational engineering and science.

Purpose and Usage

1. **MATLAB**:

   – MATLAB is primarily a numerical computing environment and programming language.

   – It is used for data analysis, algorithm development, mathematical modeling, and general-purpose programming.

   – MATLAB scripts and functions are written to execute numerical and symbolic computations.

1. **Simulink**:

   – Simulink, on the other hand, is a graphical simulation and modeling tool.

– It is designed for modeling dynamic systems, simulating their behavior, and analyzing their responses.

– Simulink models are graphical representations of systems using blocks and connections.

Modeling Paradigm

1. **MATLAB**:

– MATLAB uses a text-based scripting language to define algorithms and perform computations.

– Users write code to execute calculations, create plots, and solve mathematical problems.

1. **Simulink**:

– Simulink employs a visual, block-diagram-based approach to model systems.

– Users build models by dragging and connecting blocks that represent components or operations.

Representation of Systems

1. **MATLAB**:

– In MATLAB, systems and algorithms are represented as mathematical equations and code.

– It is suitable for mathematical modeling and algorithm development but less intuitive for system-level modeling.

1. **Simulink**:

– Simulink excels at modeling complex dynamic systems visually.

– Systems are represented as interconnected blocks, making it ideal for control systems, signal processing, and simulations.

Simulation and Analysis

1. **MATLAB**:

– MATLAB provides simulation capabilities, but they are typically used for mathematical and algorithmic simulations.

– Simulations are coded within MATLAB scripts or functions.

1. **Simulink**:

– Simulink is dedicated to system simulation and analysis.

– It offers a wide range of simulation tools and solvers optimized for dynamic systems.

Customization and Extensibility

1. **MATLAB**:

– MATLAB is highly customizable and extensible through the creation of custom functions and toolboxes.

– Users can implement their algorithms and customize the MATLAB environment.

1. **Simulink**:

– Simulink is extensible through the development of custom blocks and libraries.

– Users can create custom blocks to represent specialized components or behaviors.

Target Applications

1. **MATLAB**:

– MATLAB is used for a broad spectrum of applications, including data analysis, image processing, machine learning, and more.

– It is suitable for tasks that require numerical computation and algorithm development.

1. **Simulink**:

– Simulink is employed for modeling and simulating dynamic systems, particularly in control systems engineering, aerospace, automotive, and signal processing.

– It excels in scenarios where systems need to be simulated and analyzed in a dynamic, time-dependent manner.

Integration

1. **MATLAB**:

- MATLAB and Simulink are tightly integrated.

- Users can call MATLAB functions from Simulink models and vice versa, facilitating a seamless workflow when both tools are needed.

IN CONCLUSION, WHILE MATLAB and Simulink are both valuable tools in the engineering and scientific communities, they serve different purposes. MATLAB is a versatile numerical computing environment and programming language, while Simulink specializes in modeling, simulating, and analyzing dynamic systems through a graphical block-diagram approach. Understanding their distinctions will help you choose the right tool for your specific computational needs.

6.3. Basic Simulink Models

IN SIMULINK, MODELS are built using a graphical block-diagram approach, making it a powerful tool for visualizing and simulating dynamic systems. In this section, we will explore the basics of creating Simulink models, including the use of blocks, connections, and configuration settings.

Blocks in Simulink

BLOCKS ARE FUNDAMENTAL building components in Simulink models. Each block represents a specific operation, mathematical function, or system component. Simulink provides an extensive library of predefined blocks categorized by domain, such as mathematics, signal processing, control systems, and more. Users can drag and drop blocks from the library onto the Simulink canvas to create their models.

Connecting Blocks

ONCE BLOCKS ARE PLACED on the canvas, they are connected to represent the flow of data or signals between them. Connections are made by clicking and dragging from one block's output port to another block's input port. The direction of the connection arrow indicates the flow of data or signals. For example, a signal flows from the output to the input of a block.

Parameters and Block Configuration

BLOCKS IN SIMULINK have configurable parameters that determine their behavior. Double-clicking on a block opens its configuration dialog, where users can set parameters such as initial conditions, sample time, and block-specific settings. These parameters define how the block interacts with other blocks and the system as a whole.

Simulink Canvas

THE SIMULINK CANVAS is the workspace where users create, arrange, and connect blocks to build their models. Users can zoom in and out to adjust the level of detail, and they can organize blocks to enhance the model's clarity. The canvas provides a visual representation of the system being modeled, making it easier to understand and debug.

Example: Simple Mass-Spring-Damper System

LET'S CREATE A SIMPLE Simulink model to illustrate these concepts. We'll model a mass-spring-damper system, a classic example in control systems engineering.

1. **Adding Blocks**:

   – Drag and drop the "Sum" block, "Gain" block, and "Integrator" block from the Simulink library onto the canvas.

1. **Connecting Blocks**:

   – Connect the output of the "Sum" block to the input of the "Gain" block.

   – Connect the output of the "Gain" block to the input of the "Integrator" block.

1. **Configuring Blocks**:

   – Double-click on the "Gain" block and set its gain value to 5.

   – Double-click on the "Integrator" block and set its initial condition to 0.

1. **Adding Input**:

   – Drag and drop the "Step" block from the library onto the canvas.

   – Connect the output of the "Step" block to the input of the "Sum" block.

– Double-click on the "Step" block and set its "Time" to start at 0 and change to 1 at 1 second.

1. **Simulation**:

– Configure simulation parameters, such as simulation time and solver options, in the Simulink model settings.

– Run the simulation to observe the response of the mass-spring-damper system.

This simple example demonstrates how to create a basic Simulink model, connect blocks, set parameters, and simulate the system's behavior. Simulink's visual approach makes it accessible for modeling and simulating complex dynamic systems in various domains, from control systems to signal processing and beyond.

6.4. Simulating Dynamic Systems

SIMULINK IS WIDELY used for simulating dynamic systems in various engineering and scientific domains. In this section, we will delve into the process of simulating dynamic systems using Simulink, including setting up simulations, defining input signals, and analyzing simulation results.

Setting Up Simulations

1. **Model Configuration**:

– Before simulating a dynamic system, you need to configure your Simulink model. This involves specifying simulation time, solver settings, and other parameters relevant to your system.

– Simulation settings can be adjusted in the model's Configuration Parameters dialog, accessible through the "Model" menu.

1. **Solver Selection**:

– Simulink offers different solvers to handle various types of systems and simulation scenarios. The choice of solver depends on factors like system complexity, stiff equations, and real-time simulation requirements.

– Common solver options include the variable-step ODE solvers, fixed-step solvers, and real-time solvers.

Defining Input Signals

1. **Signal Sources**:

– To simulate a dynamic system, you typically need to provide input signals that drive the system's behavior.

– Simulink provides various blocks for generating input signals, such as the "Step," "Ramp," and "Sinewave" blocks.

1. **External Input Data**:

– Simulink allows you to import external data into your simulation. This can be useful for performing simulations based on real-world data or measurements.

– External data can be imported from files, MATLAB workspace variables, or external hardware.

Simulating the System

1. **Simulation Execution**:

– To run a simulation, simply click the "Run" button in the Simulink model window.

– Simulink will execute the model based on the configured simulation settings and input signals.

1. **Real-Time Simulation**:

– Simulink supports real-time simulation, which is essential for applications like hardware-in-the-loop (HIL) testing and control system validation.

– Real-time simulation requires appropriate hardware and drivers to ensure accurate timing and response.

Analyzing Simulation Results

1. **Scope Blocks**:

– Simulink provides scope blocks that allow you to visualize and analyze simulation results in real-time.

– You can add scope blocks to your model and connect them to signals of interest for monitoring.

1. **Simulation Data Logging**:

– Simulink can log simulation data, which can be reviewed and analyzed after the simulation run.

– Logged data can be exported to MATLAB for further analysis and post-processing.

Example: Pendulum Simulation

LET'S CONSIDER A SIMPLE example of simulating a pendulum system using Simulink. The pendulum's motion can be described by differential equations, and Simulink can help us visualize its behavior.

1. **Model Setup**:

– Create a Simulink model and set up the necessary parameters, such as simulation time and solver options.

1. **System Modeling**:

– Define the mathematical equations that govern the pendulum's motion using Simulink blocks. This may involve creating custom blocks or using predefined blocks for modeling.

1. **Input Signal**:

– Create an input signal that represents an initial disturbance or force applied to the pendulum.

1. **Simulation Run**:

– Execute the simulation to observe the pendulum's motion over time.

1. **Results Analysis**:

– Analyze the simulation results to understand the pendulum's behavior, including its oscillations and stability.

Simulink's capabilities for simulating dynamic systems make it a valuable tool for engineers and scientists working on a wide range of applications, from mechanical systems like pendulums to complex control systems and beyond. It enables the exploration of system behavior without the need for physical prototypes, facilitating efficient design and analysis.

6.5. Simulink for Control Systems

SIMULINK IS A POWERFUL tool for designing, simulating, and analyzing control systems across various industries, including aerospace, automotive, robotics, and more. In this section, we will explore how Simulink is used for control system design and analysis.

Control System Modeling

1. **Transfer Functions and State-Space Representation**:

– Control systems are often represented using transfer functions or state-space models. Simulink allows you to model these systems using blocks that represent transfer functions, integrators, summing junctions, and more.

– You can build your control system model by connecting these blocks on the Simulink canvas.

1. **Custom Block Creation**:

– For complex control systems or unique requirements, you can create custom blocks in Simulink using

MATLAB code or the Simulink block authoring tools. This flexibility enables you to model control systems specific to your application.

Controller Design

1. **PID Controllers**:

– Simulink includes blocks for designing Proportional-Integral-Derivative (PID) controllers, which are widely used in control systems.

– You can configure PID controllers by setting parameters like gains and time constants.

1. **Frequency Domain Design**:

– Simulink offers tools for designing controllers in the frequency domain. You can use the Control System Toolbox for tasks like root locus analysis and Bode plot design.

Simulation and Analysis

1. **Closed-Loop Simulation**:

– Simulink allows you to perform closed-loop simulations, where the control system's response to disturbances and reference inputs can be analyzed.

– Simulations help you evaluate the performance of your control system under various conditions.

1. **Time and Frequency Domain Analysis**:

– You can analyze control system behavior in both the time and frequency domains using Simulink. Time-domain analysis includes step response, impulse response, and settling time calculations. Frequency-domain analysis involves Bode plots and Nyquist plots.

Control System Tuning

1. **Automated Tuning Tools**:

– Simulink offers automated tuning tools like the Control System Tuner app, which assists in tuning controller parameters for optimal performance.

1. **Manual Tuning**:

– Engineers can manually fine-tune controller parameters in Simulink by adjusting gains and observing the system's response in real-time.

Real-Time Testing and Hardware-in-the-Loop (HIL)

1. **Real-Time Simulation**:

– Simulink supports real-time testing of control systems, which is crucial for validating control algorithms and ensuring they work correctly in real-world scenarios.

1. **HIL Testing**:

– Hardware-in-the-loop (HIL) testing involves connecting physical hardware, such as sensors and actuators, to a Simulink model to test control algorithms in a realistic environment.

– Simulink Real-Time and Simulink Desktop Real-Time products facilitate HIL testing.

Example: Quadcopter Control

CONSIDER THE CONTROL system design for a quadcopter, a popular application in robotics and aerospace.

1. **Modeling**:

– Create a Simulink model representing the quadcopter's dynamics, including its sensors, actuators, and control algorithms.

1. **Controller Design**:

– Design controllers, such as a PID controller, to stabilize and control the quadcopter's position and orientation.

1. **Simulation**:

– Perform closed-loop simulations to assess the quadcopter's response to control inputs and external disturbances.

1. **Tuning**:

– Tune controller gains to optimize the quadcopter's performance in terms of stability, agility, and responsiveness.

1. **Real-Time Testing**:

   – Connect physical sensors and actuators to the Simulink model to perform hardware-in-the-loop testing and validate the control system's performance.

Simulink's comprehensive capabilities make it an essential tool for control system engineers, enabling them to design, simulate, and fine-tune control systems with precision and efficiency. Whether you're working on aerospace control, automotive systems, or robotics, Simulink provides the flexibility and tools needed for successful control system development.

Chapter 7: Specialized MATLAB Toolboxes

7.1. Image Processing Toolbox

THE IMAGE PROCESSING Toolbox in MATLAB is a comprehensive set of tools and functions designed for performing various operations on digital images. It offers a wide range of capabilities, from basic image manipulation to advanced image analysis and computer vision tasks. In this section, we will explore the key features and functionalities of the Image Processing Toolbox.

Basic Image Operations

1. **Image Loading and Display**:

- The toolbox provides functions for reading and displaying images in various formats, including JPEG, PNG, and BMP.

- You can use the imread function to load an image and imshow to display it.

1. **Image Enhancement**:

- Enhance the visual quality of images through operations like contrast adjustment, histogram equalization, and sharpening.

- Functions like imadjust, histeq, and imsharpen are commonly used for image enhancement.

Filtering and Noise Reduction

1. **Filtering Operations**:

– Apply various filters to images for tasks such as blurring, edge detection, and noise reduction.

– Functions like imfilter and fspecial allow you to create custom filters and apply them to images.

1. **Noise Reduction**:

– Remove noise from images using techniques like median filtering and Gaussian filtering.

– The toolbox provides functions such as medfilt2 and imgaussfilt for noise reduction.

Image Segmentation

1. **Segmentation Algorithms**:

– Divide an image into meaningful regions or objects using segmentation algorithms like thresholding, region growing, and watershed.

– Functions like imbinarize, regiongrowing, and watershed aid in image segmentation.

Morphological Operations

1. **Erosion and Dilation**:

– Morphological operations, such as erosion and dilation, are useful for modifying the shape and structure of objects in binary images.

– Functions like imerode and imdilate perform these operations.

1. **Opening and Closing**:

– Opening and closing operations are employed for tasks like noise removal and object connectivity.

– Functions like imopen and imclose combine erosion and dilation operations.

Object Analysis and Measurements

1. **Object Properties**:

– Calculate properties of objects in binary images, such as area, perimeter, centroid, and bounding box.

– Functions like regionprops provide a range of object measurements.

1. **Blob Analysis**:

– Perform blob analysis to identify and analyze regions of interest in an image.

– The toolbox offers functions like bwconncomp and labelmatrix for blob analysis.

Advanced Image Processing

1. **Image Registration**:

– Align and register images from different sources or time points.

– Functions like imregister and imwarp assist in image registration.

1. **Image Restoration**:

– Restore degraded or blurred images using techniques like deconvolution.

– The toolbox includes functions like deconvblind for image restoration.

Computer Vision and Machine Learning

1. **Object Detection**:

– Detect objects or features within images using techniques like template matching and Hough transforms.

– Functions like imfindcircles and vision.TemplateMatcher enable object detection.

1. **Deep Learning Integration**:

– Integrate deep learning models and frameworks with the Image Processing Toolbox for advanced computer vision tasks.

– You can use the Deep Learning Toolbox in conjunction with the Image Processing Toolbox for tasks like object recognition and image classification.

THE IMAGE PROCESSING Toolbox in MATLAB is a valuable resource for researchers, engineers, and scientists working in fields such as image analysis, computer vision, medical imaging, and remote sensing. Its extensive set of functions and capabilities simplifies complex image processing tasks and facilitates the development of innovative image-based solutions. Whether you need to enhance, segment, or analyze images, this toolbox provides the tools and flexibility to accomplish your goals efficiently.

7.2. Signal Processing Toolbox

THE SIGNAL PROCESSING Toolbox in MATLAB is a powerful collection of functions and tools designed for working with signals and systems. Signals can be found in various domains, including audio, image, sensor data, and communications. This toolbox provides a wide range of capabilities for processing, analyzing, and visualizing signals. In this section, we will explore the key features and functionalities of the Signal Processing Toolbox.

Signal Analysis

1. **Signal Representation**:

– MATLAB's Signal Processing Toolbox allows you to represent signals, such as audio waveforms, using arrays or vectors.

– Common signal types include continuous-time signals, discrete-time signals, and digital signals.

1. **Signal Visualization:**

– Visualize signals using functions like plot, stem, and spectrogram to gain insights into their characteristics.

– The toolbox offers numerous plot customization options for displaying signals effectively.

Filtering and Filtering Design

1. **Filter Design:**

– Design digital filters, including low-pass, high-pass, band-pass, and band-stop filters, using various design methods such as Butterworth, Chebyshev, and elliptic.

– Functions like butter, cheby1, and ellip assist in filter design.

1. **Filtering Operations:**

– Apply digital filters to signals for tasks like noise reduction, frequency-domain transformations, and signal conditioning.

– Use functions like filter, conv, and freqz for filtering operations.

Spectral Analysis

1. **Frequency Domain Analysis:**

– Analyze signals in the frequency domain to understand their spectral characteristics.

– Functions like fft (Fast Fourier Transform) and periodogram allow you to compute power spectral density and frequency components.

1. **Spectral Visualization**:

– Visualize frequency content using functions like spectrogram and pwelch for time-frequency analysis and spectrograms.

Time-Frequency Analysis

1. **Wavelet Transform**:

– Perform time-frequency analysis using the continuous and discrete wavelet transforms.

– Functions like cwt and wavedec enable wavelet analysis.

1. **Short-Time Fourier Transform (STFT)**:

– Compute STFT representations of signals to analyze how signal frequencies change over time.

– The toolbox provides stft and istft functions for STFT analysis.

Filter Banks and Multirate Signal Processing

1. **Filter Banks**:

– Implement filter banks for tasks like audio compression (e.g., MP3) and signal decomposition.

– Functions like modwt (Maximal Overlap Discrete Wavelet Transform) support filter bank applications.

Signal Processing for Communications

1. **Modulation and Demodulation**:

– Design and analyze modulation schemes such as amplitude modulation (AM), frequency modulation (FM), and phase-shift keying (PSK).

– Functions like ammod and pskmod assist in modulation and demodulation.

1. **Channel Modeling**:

– Simulate communication channels and evaluate their impact on signal quality.

– The toolbox includes functions for channel modeling and signal impairment analysis.

Real-World Applications

1. **Audio Signal Processing**:

– Process and analyze audio signals for applications like speech recognition, audio compression, and music analysis.

– MATLAB's Signal Processing Toolbox is commonly used in audio processing.

1. **Image and Video Processing**:

– Apply signal processing techniques to images and videos for tasks such as image enhancement, denoising, and compression.

– The toolbox integrates with the Image Processing Toolbox for comprehensive image and video analysis.

1. **Sensor Data Processing**:

– Process sensor data from various sources, including accelerometers, gyroscopes, and environmental sensors.

– Signal processing helps extract meaningful information from sensor readings.

THE SIGNAL PROCESSING Toolbox in MATLAB is an essential resource for engineers, researchers, and scientists working in fields such as telecommunications, audio processing, biomedical signal analysis, and more. Its wide range of functions simplifies complex signal processing tasks, making it easier to analyze and manipulate signals in various domains. Whether you're working with audio, sensor data, or communication signals, this toolbox provides the tools and flexibility needed to accomplish your signal processing objectives efficiently.

7.3. Financial Toolbox

THE FINANCIAL TOOLBOX in MATLAB is a specialized collection of functions and tools designed for financial modeling, risk analysis, and portfolio management. It provides the necessary resources for professionals in finance, investment, and risk management to model financial instruments, perform risk assessments, and optimize investment portfolios. In this section, we will explore the key features and functionalities of the Financial Toolbox.

Financial Instruments

1. **Financial Data Retrieval**:

– The Financial Toolbox allows you to retrieve financial market data, including historical price and volume information for stocks, bonds, and other financial instruments.

– Functions like fetch and getdata enable data retrieval from various financial data providers.

1. **Interest Rate Modeling**:

– Model and analyze interest rate instruments, including bonds, fixed-income securities, and derivatives.

– The toolbox provides functions for interest rate curve modeling and yield curve bootstrapping.

Risk Assessment and Management

1. **Risk Metrics**:

– Calculate risk measures such as value-at-risk (VaR), conditional value-at-risk (CVaR), and risk-adjusted performance metrics.

– Functions like var and cvar assist in risk assessment.

1. **Portfolio Optimization**:

– Optimize investment portfolios to achieve desired risk-return profiles using mean-variance analysis and other optimization techniques.

– The toolbox includes functions like portopt for portfolio optimization.

Financial Modeling

1. **Option Pricing**:

– Model and price various financial options, including European, American, and exotic options.

– Functions like blsprice and binprice provide option pricing capabilities.

1. **Credit Risk Modeling**:

– Evaluate credit risk and model credit derivatives using credit risk models.

– Functions for credit risk modeling include defprob and creditrisk.

Time Series Analysis

1. **Time Series Modeling**:

– Analyze and model time series data for financial applications.

– Functions like arima and garch support time series modeling and forecasting.

Financial Economics

1. **Capital Asset Pricing Model (CAPM)**:

– Calculate asset and portfolio beta, expected returns, and risk-adjusted performance based on the CAPM framework.

– The toolbox offers functions for CAPM analysis.

1. **Black-Scholes Model**:

– Implement the Black-Scholes model for pricing European options and understanding option sensitivities (Greeks).

– Functions like blsprice and greeks assist in Black-Scholes calculations.

Real-World Applications

1. **Investment Analysis**:

– Perform financial analysis and investment evaluation, including net present value (NPV), internal rate of return (IRR), and cash flow modeling.

– MATLAB's Financial Toolbox is commonly used for investment analysis.

1. **Risk Management**:

– Assess and manage risks associated with financial instruments, portfolios, and derivatives.

– The toolbox supports various risk management tasks, including stress testing and scenario analysis.

1. **Portfolio Management**:

– Optimize investment portfolios, rebalance assets, and assess portfolio performance.

– Professionals in portfolio management rely on the toolbox for portfolio optimization and analysis.

1. **Financial Research and Analysis**:

– Conduct financial research, analyze market data, and develop financial models for research purposes.

– The toolbox provides tools for financial research and data analysis.

THE FINANCIAL TOOLBOX in MATLAB is an indispensable resource for financial analysts, economists, investment professionals, and risk managers. Its comprehensive set of functions and capabilities simplifies complex financial modeling, risk assessment, and investment analysis tasks. Whether you're pricing options, managing portfolios, or evaluating investment strategies, this toolbox offers the tools and flexibility needed to accomplish your financial modeling objectives efficiently and accurately.

7.4. Robotics Toolbox

THE ROBOTICS TOOLBOX in MATLAB is a specialized collection of functions and tools designed for robotic system modeling, simulation, and control. It provides a comprehensive set of resources for researchers, engineers, and students working in the field of robotics, enabling them to model robots, perform kinematic and dynamic analysis, and develop control strategies. In this section, we will explore the key features and functionalities of the Robotics Toolbox.

Robot Modeling

1. **Robot Description**:

– The Robotics Toolbox allows you to describe robotic systems by specifying the robot's kinematic structure, including links, joints, and end-effectors.

– You can create robot models using the SerialLink class, which represents serial-link manipulators.

1. **Forward Kinematics**:

– Calculate the end-effector pose (position and orientation) given joint angles using forward kinematics.

– Functions like fkine enable forward kinematics computations.

1. **Inverse Kinematics**:

– Solve inverse kinematics problems to find joint angles that achieve a desired end-effector pose.

– The toolbox provides functions like ikine for inverse kinematics.

Robot Control

1. **Trajectory Generation**:

– Generate trajectories for robot motion, such as linear and circular paths.

– Functions like mtraj assist in trajectory generation.

1. **Inverse Dynamics**:

– Compute the joint torques required to achieve a desired end-effector motion.

– The toolbox provides functions for inverse dynamics calculations.

1. **Robot Control Algorithms**:

– Implement control algorithms for robot manipulation tasks, including joint-space and Cartesian-space control.

– You can design custom control strategies or use predefined control functions.

Kinematic and Dynamic Analysis

1. **Robot Kinematics**:

– Analyze the kinematic properties of robotic systems, including joint velocities and Jacobian matrices.

– Functions like jacob0 and ikine support kinematic analysis.

1. **Robot Dynamics**:

– Perform dynamic analysis to compute joint torques and accelerations for given motion trajectories.

– The toolbox includes functions for dynamic modeling and analysis.

Visualization and Simulation

1. **3D Visualization**:

– Visualize robotic systems and their motion in a 3D environment.

– The toolbox integrates with MATLAB's 3D visualization capabilities for realistic robot visualization.

1. **Simulation**:

– Simulate robot motion and control strategies to test and evaluate robotic algorithms.

– Functions like fkine and robot.plot enable simulation of robot motion.

Real-World Applications

1. **Robotics Research**:

– Researchers in robotics use the toolbox for modeling and analyzing robotic systems, as well as developing control algorithms.

1. **Robotics Education**:

– Educators and students use the Robotics Toolbox to learn and teach robotics concepts, including kinematics, dynamics, and control.

1. **Robotics Development**:

– Engineers and developers use MATLAB's Robotics Toolbox to prototype and test robotic systems and control algorithms.

1. **Robotics Simulations**:

– Simulate real-world robotic scenarios for applications in manufacturing, automation, and autonomous robotics.

THE ROBOTICS TOOLBOX in MATLAB is a valuable resource for anyone involved in the field of robotics, from researchers and educators to engineers and developers. Its capabilities for modeling, analyzing, and controlling robotic systems make it an essential tool for designing and testing robotic algorithms and applications. Whether you're working on robot control strategies, studying kinematics and dynamics, or developing robotic simulations, this toolbox offers the flexibility and functionality needed to advance your work in the field of robotics.

7.5. Machine Learning Toolbox

THE MACHINE LEARNING Toolbox in MATLAB is a comprehensive set of tools and functions that empower users to develop, implement, and deploy machine learning models and algorithms. With this toolbox, you can perform a wide range of tasks, from data preprocessing to model training and evaluation. In this section, we will delve into the key features and functionalities of the Machine Learning Toolbox.

Data Preprocessing

1. **Data Cleaning and Transformation**:

- Prepare and preprocess raw data by handling missing values, outliers, and noise.

- Functions like fillmissing and normalize assist in data preprocessing.

1. **Feature Engineering**:

- Create meaningful features from raw data to improve model performance.

- The toolbox provides tools for feature selection and transformation.

Supervised Learning

1. **Classification**:

- Train classification models to categorize data into predefined classes or labels.

- Algorithms such as decision trees, support vector machines, and neural networks are available.

1. **Regression**:

– Develop regression models to predict numerical values or continuous outcomes.

– Tools for linear regression, polynomial regression, and ensemble regression are included.

Unsupervised Learning

1. **Clustering**:

– Use clustering algorithms to group data points into clusters based on similarities.

– K-means clustering and hierarchical clustering are supported.

1. **Dimensionality Reduction**:

– Reduce the dimensionality of high-dimensional data while preserving its important features.

– Principal Component Analysis (PCA) and t-distributed Stochastic Neighbor Embedding (t-SNE) are examples.

Deep Learning

1. **Neural Networks**:

– Design and train deep neural networks for various tasks, including image classification and natural language processing.

– MATLAB's deep learning capabilities support popular frameworks like TensorFlow and PyTorch.

1. **Transfer Learning**:

– Leverage pretrained deep learning models and fine-tune them for specific applications.

– The toolbox simplifies transfer learning workflows.

Model Evaluation

1. **Cross-Validation**:

– Perform cross-validation to assess model performance and reduce overfitting.

– Functions like crossval facilitate cross-validation procedures.

1. **Model Metrics**:

– Calculate various metrics, including accuracy, precision, recall, and F1-score, to evaluate model performance.

– The toolbox provides metrics for classification and regression.

Deployment and Integration

1. **Code Generation**:

– Generate C/C++ code or deploy models as standalone applications or web services.

– This allows integration of machine learning models into other software and systems.

1. **Integration with Other Tools**:

– MATLAB's Machine Learning Toolbox can be integrated with other MATLAB toolboxes and external libraries for comprehensive data analysis.

Real-World Applications

1. **Data Analytics**:

– Use machine learning to gain insights from data, make predictions, and drive data-driven decisions in various industries.

1. **Image and Video Processing**:

– Apply machine learning models for tasks like image recognition, object detection, and video analysis.

1. **Natural Language Processing (NLP)**:

– Implement NLP models for text classification, sentiment analysis, and language translation.

1. **Predictive Maintenance**:

– Predict equipment failures and maintenance needs in industrial settings.

1. **Financial Modeling**:

– Develop predictive models for financial markets, risk assessment, and fraud detection.

1. **Healthcare**:

– Apply machine learning to medical image analysis, disease prediction, and patient monitoring.

THE MACHINE LEARNING Toolbox in MATLAB is a powerful resource for data scientists, researchers, and engineers. Its extensive capabilities make it suitable for a wide range of applications, from image recognition to financial modeling and predictive maintenance. Whether you're new to machine learning or an experienced practitioner, this toolbox offers the tools and flexibility needed to tackle complex machine learning tasks and build robust predictive models.

Chapter 8: Scientific Computing with MATLAB

8.1. Computational Biology

COMPUTATIONAL BIOLOGY is a multidisciplinary field that combines biology, computer science, mathematics, and statistics to analyze and model biological data. MATLAB plays a pivotal role in this domain by providing a robust environment for conducting various computational biology tasks. In this section, we will explore the applications of MATLAB in computational biology, highlighting key tools, techniques, and resources available.

Sequence Analysis

1. **Sequence Manipulation**:

   – MATLAB offers functions and toolboxes for reading, writing, and manipulating biological sequences, including DNA, RNA, and protein sequences.

   – Common operations like sequence alignment, translation, and reverse complementation are easily performed.

1. **Sequence Database Access**:

   – Access online biological sequence databases and retrieve sequences for analysis.

   – The Bioinformatics Toolbox provides interfaces to popular databases like GenBank and UniProt.

Genomic Data Analysis

1. **Genome Assembly and Annotation**:

– MATLAB aids in the assembly and annotation of genomes, which is crucial for understanding genetic structures.

– Tools like Bioinformatics Toolbox and third-party packages facilitate these tasks.

1. **Gene Expression Analysis**:

– Analyze gene expression data using techniques such as microarray analysis and RNA-seq.

– Perform differential gene expression analysis and identify biomarkers.

Protein Structure and Function

1. **Protein Structure Prediction**:

– Predict protein structures and perform structure-function relationship studies.

– The toolbox allows for molecular dynamics simulations and protein structure visualization.

1. **Protein-Protein Interaction Analysis**:

– Investigate protein-protein interactions and build interaction networks.

– Identify protein complexes and study their functional implications.

Systems Biology

1. **Mathematical Modeling**:

– Create mathematical models of biological systems using MATLAB's modeling and simulation capabilities.

– Simulate and analyze dynamic processes in biological systems.

1. **Pathway Analysis**:

– Explore biological pathways and signaling networks to gain insights into cellular processes.

– Tools like SimBiology and the Systems Biology Toolbox support pathway analysis.

Data Visualization

1. **Biological Data Visualization**:

– Visualize biological data, such as sequence alignments, phylogenetic trees, and protein structures.

– MATLAB's plotting and visualization capabilities are useful for creating informative graphics.

1. **Interactive Dashboards**:

– Build interactive dashboards for exploring and presenting biological data to researchers and stakeholders.

Resources and Toolboxes

1. **Bioinformatics Toolbox**:

– This toolbox offers a wide range of functions and algorithms for sequence analysis, genomics, and structural biology.

1. **Systems Biology Toolbox**:

– Designed for modeling and simulating dynamic biological systems, it supports ordinary differential equations (ODEs) and stochastic simulations.

1. **Biological Data Integration**:

– Integrate biological data from various sources, such as genomics, proteomics, and metabolomics, for comprehensive analysis.

Real-World Applications

1. **Drug Discovery**:

– MATLAB is employed in drug discovery by modeling the interactions between drugs and biological targets.

1. **Cancer Research**:

– Researchers use MATLAB for analyzing cancer genomics data, identifying biomarkers, and developing personalized treatments.

1. **Phylogenetics**:

– Construct phylogenetic trees to study evolutionary relationships among species.

1. **Neuroscience**:

– MATLAB is utilized in neuroscience research for modeling neural networks and analyzing brain imaging data.

IN CONCLUSION, MATLAB serves as a versatile tool in computational biology, enabling researchers to tackle complex biological questions, analyze large datasets, and develop predictive models. Its extensive toolboxes and capabilities make it a valuable resource for advancing our understanding of the biological world and addressing critical challenges in fields like drug discovery, genomics, and systems biology.

8.2. Chemical Engineering Applications

MATLAB IS WIDELY USED in chemical engineering for modeling, simulating, and analyzing complex chemical processes. It provides a powerful platform for solving differential equations, optimizing processes, and visualizing results. In this section, we will explore some of the key applications of MATLAB in chemical engineering.

Process Modeling and Simulation

1. **Reaction Kinetics**:

– MATLAB allows chemical engineers to model reaction kinetics using ordinary differential equations (ODEs) or partial differential equations (PDEs).

– The ability to define complex reaction mechanisms and boundary conditions simplifies the study of chemical reactions.

1. **Heat and Mass Transfer**:

– Simulate heat and mass transfer processes in chemical reactors and unit operations.

– MATLAB's numerical solvers are valuable for solving heat conduction, convection, and diffusion problems.

1. **Process Dynamics**:

– Analyze the dynamic behavior of chemical processes using control system tools in MATLAB.

– Design and tune controllers for maintaining process stability.

Optimization and Design

1. **Process Optimization**:

– MATLAB offers optimization algorithms that help engineers find optimal operating conditions.

– Perform sensitivity analysis and parameter estimation to improve process efficiency.

1. **Experimental Design**:

– Design experiments and analyze data to optimize processes and discover optimal parameter settings.

Data Analysis and Visualization

1. **Data Processing**:

– Import and preprocess data from sensors and experiments for analysis.

– Handle noisy data, filter signals, and perform statistical analysis.

1. **Visualization**:

– Create informative plots and graphs to visualize process variables, trends, and results.

– MATLAB's plotting capabilities allow for customizing and annotating figures.

Chemical Engineering Toolboxes

1. **Chemical Reaction Engineering Toolbox**:

– Specialized toolbox for modeling and simulating chemical reactions, including reaction kinetics and reactor design.

1. **Partial Differential Equation Toolbox**:

– Useful for solving PDEs that arise in modeling transport phenomena in chemical processes.

1. **Optimization Toolbox**:

– Provides a wide range of optimization algorithms for solving complex optimization problems.

Real-World Applications

1. **Chemical Process Design**:

– Engineers use MATLAB to design and optimize chemical processes, from reaction kinetics to equipment sizing.

1. **Process Control**:

– Employ MATLAB for designing control systems that maintain desired process conditions and improve safety.

1. **Environmental Engineering**:

– MATLAB aids in modeling and analyzing environmental processes, including air and water quality.

1. **Materials Science**:

– Chemical engineers use MATLAB to study material properties, phase diagrams, and crystallization processes.

1. **Bioprocess Engineering**:

- In biotechnology, MATLAB helps in modeling and optimizing bioprocesses for producing pharmaceuticals and biofuels.

IN SUMMARY, MATLAB is a versatile tool for chemical engineers, providing a wide range of capabilities for modeling, simulating, and optimizing chemical processes. Its extensive toolbox ecosystem and numerical solvers make it an essential resource for tackling complex challenges in chemical engineering, from reaction kinetics to process control and environmental applications.

8.3. Physics Simulations

MATLAB IS A POWERFUL tool for conducting physics simulations, allowing researchers and physicists to explore various physical phenomena and analyze complex systems. In this section, we will delve into the applications of MATLAB in physics simulations.

Numerical Simulations

1. **Classical Mechanics:**

- MATLAB is commonly used to simulate the motion of particles and rigid bodies under the influence of forces and constraints.

- Engineers and physicists can study concepts like projectile motion, orbital dynamics, and harmonic oscillations.

1. **Quantum Mechanics:**

– MATLAB facilitates the numerical solution of Schrödinger's equation for quantum systems.

– Researchers can explore quantum states, energy levels, and wave functions.

1. **Electromagnetism**:

– Simulate electromagnetic phenomena, including electric and magnetic fields, using MATLAB's finite element analysis capabilities.

– Study concepts like electromagnetic waves, antenna design, and magnetostatics.

Computational Physics

1. **Particle Physics**:

– Researchers in particle physics use MATLAB to analyze data from particle accelerators and conduct Monte Carlo simulations.

– Study high-energy particle interactions and discover new particles.

1. **Astrophysics and Cosmology**:

– Model astronomical phenomena such as gravitational interactions, stellar evolution, and cosmological simulations.

– Analyze observational data from telescopes and satellites.

1. **Fluid Dynamics**:

– MATLAB is employed to simulate fluid flow, turbulence, and heat transfer in a wide range of applications, from aerodynamics to weather modeling.

Mathematical Tools

1. **Differential Equations**:

– MATLAB's differential equation solvers are crucial for simulating dynamic systems in physics.

– Researchers can model physical systems using ordinary or partial differential equations.

1. **Finite Element Analysis**:

– Engineers and physicists utilize MATLAB for finite element analysis to solve partial differential equations in complex geometries.

Visualization and Analysis

1. **Data Visualization**:

– Create 2D and 3D visualizations of physical systems and their behaviors.

– MATLAB's plotting and visualization tools help in presenting results effectively.

1. **Data Analysis**:

– Analyze simulation data, extract meaningful insights, and perform statistical analysis.

– MATLAB's scripting capabilities enable automation of data analysis tasks.

Computational Tools and Toolboxes

1. **Simulink**:

– MATLAB's companion software, Simulink, is employed for modeling and simulating dynamic physical systems.

– Control engineers use Simulink for designing control systems for various applications.

1. **Image Processing Toolbox**:

– Useful for analyzing and processing images obtained from experiments or simulations.

Real-World Applications

1. **Materials Science**:

– Physicists and materials scientists use MATLAB to model material properties, conduct molecular dynamics simulations, and study phase transitions.

1. **Nuclear Physics**:

– MATLAB assists in modeling nuclear reactions, radioactive decay, and nuclear structure.

1. **Condensed Matter Physics**:

- Researchers in condensed matter physics employ MATLAB for simulating electron behavior in solid-state materials.

1. **Astrophysical Modeling**:

- MATLAB is crucial for modeling celestial objects, gravitational interactions, and the evolution of galaxies and stars.

IN SUMMARY, MATLAB serves as a valuable tool for physicists and researchers involved in physics simulations. Its computational capabilities, numerical solvers, and visualization tools enable the study of a wide range of physical phenomena, from classical mechanics to quantum physics and astrophysics. MATLAB empowers scientists to gain insights into complex physical systems and validate theoretical models through simulations and data analysis.

8.4. Mathematics and Computational Algorithms

MATHEMATICS PLAYS A fundamental role in scientific research and engineering, and MATLAB is a powerful tool for mathematical computations and algorithm development. In this section, we will explore the various ways MATLAB can be used in mathematical and computational contexts.

Mathematical Computations

1. **Symbolic Mathematics**:

– MATLAB provides a Symbolic Math Toolbox that allows for symbolic calculations. You can work with symbolic expressions, equations, and perform algebraic manipulations.

1. **Numerical Methods**:

– MATLAB offers a wide range of numerical methods for solving equations, optimizing functions, and performing root-finding tasks.

– Common numerical methods include Newton-Raphson, bisection, and gradient-based optimization.

1. **Linear Algebra**:

– MATLAB is renowned for its capabilities in linear algebra. You can perform operations on matrices and vectors, including matrix multiplication, inversion, and eigenvalue calculations.

Computational Algorithms

1. **Algorithm Development**:

– MATLAB's programming environment is ideal for developing and testing algorithms.

– Researchers and engineers use MATLAB to prototype and implement algorithms for various applications, from image processing to data analysis.

1. **Machine Learning and Artificial Intelligence**:

- MATLAB offers toolboxes for machine learning and deep learning, making it suitable for developing and training models for predictive analytics, image recognition, and natural language processing.

1. **Optimization Algorithms**:

- Engineers and researchers use MATLAB to develop and test optimization algorithms for diverse optimization problems, including linear, nonlinear, and integer optimization.

Mathematical Modeling

1. **Simulations**:

- MATLAB is widely used for mathematical modeling and simulation of physical systems, financial models, and biological processes.

- Engineers and scientists use MATLAB to model dynamic systems using differential equations.

1. **Curve Fitting**:

- Researchers can perform curve fitting to experimental data using MATLAB's curve-fitting toolbox.

- This helps in data analysis and model parameter estimation.

Advanced Mathematical Capabilities

1. **Parallel Computing**:

– MATLAB supports parallel computing, enabling users to speed up mathematical computations by utilizing multiple processors or clusters.

1. **GPU Computing**:

– MATLAB can leverage graphics processing units (GPUs) for accelerated mathematical computations, particularly beneficial for deep learning and large-scale simulations.

Coding and Scripting

1. **Custom Functions**:

– MATLAB allows users to create custom functions and scripts for mathematical computations.

– This encourages code reuse and simplifies complex calculations.

1. **Scripting and Automation**:

– You can automate repetitive mathematical tasks in MATLAB using scripts, making it efficient for processing large datasets.

Real-World Applications

1. **Engineering**:

– MATLAB is widely used in engineering disciplines for solving complex mathematical problems, designing control systems, and conducting simulations.

1. **Finance**:

– Financial analysts and quants use MATLAB for mathematical modeling in risk management, portfolio optimization, and financial derivatives pricing.

1. **Scientific Research**:

– Scientists across various domains employ MATLAB for mathematical modeling, data analysis, and simulations in physics, chemistry, biology, and environmental science.

1. **Aerospace**:

– MATLAB is used for trajectory analysis, control system design, and simulations in the aerospace industry.

IN CONCLUSION, MATLAB serves as a versatile tool for mathematical computations and algorithm development in various fields, including engineering, finance, and scientific research. Its extensive mathematical libraries, coupled with its programming environment, enable users to tackle complex mathematical challenges, develop computational algorithms, and create mathematical models for a wide range of applications.

8.5. Environmental Science Modeling

ENVIRONMENTAL SCIENCE is a multidisciplinary field that focuses on understanding the Earth's environment, including its processes, systems, and the impact of human activities. MATLAB plays a crucial role in environmental science modeling by providing tools for data analysis, simulation, and visualization. In this section, we will explore how MATLAB is used in environmental science modeling and its applications in this field.

Data Analysis and Processing

1. **Data Import and Management**:

– MATLAB offers extensive data import capabilities, allowing environmental scientists to load and manage diverse data formats, including CSV, Excel, and databases.

– This is crucial for handling environmental data collected from various sources such as sensors, satellites, and field measurements.

1. **Data Cleaning and Preprocessing**:

– Environmental datasets often require cleaning and preprocessing to remove noise, outliers, and missing values.

– MATLAB provides functions and tools for data cleaning and transformation.

1. **Statistical Analysis**:

– Researchers in environmental science use MATLAB for statistical analysis to uncover patterns, trends, and correlations within datasets.

– Statistical tests and exploratory data analysis are commonly performed in MATLAB.

Mathematical Modeling and Simulation

1. **Numerical Simulations**:

– MATLAB is employed to simulate environmental phenomena and processes using mathematical models.

– Examples include modeling climate change, groundwater flow, and ecological systems.

1. **Differential Equations**:

– Environmental models often involve solving complex differential equations.

– MATLAB's numerical solvers are used to tackle these equations efficiently.

GIS Integration

1. **Geospatial Analysis**:

– MATLAB can be integrated with Geographic Information Systems (GIS) data and tools for geospatial analysis.

– Environmental scientists use this capability for spatial modeling and mapping.

1. **Remote Sensing**:

– MATLAB supports the processing and analysis of remote sensing data, including satellite imagery and aerial photographs.

– This is crucial for monitoring land use, vegetation, and environmental changes.

Environmental Monitoring and Management

1. **Sensors and IoT**:

– MATLAB can interface with IoT devices and sensors, enabling real-time environmental monitoring.

– Data from sensors can be analyzed, visualized, and used for decision-making in environmental management.

1. **Predictive Modeling**:

– Environmental scientists use MATLAB to build predictive models for various applications, such as predicting air quality, water quality, and natural disasters.

Visualization and Reporting

1. **Data Visualization**:

– MATLAB provides powerful tools for creating visualizations of environmental data, including 2D and 3D plots, heatmaps, and geographic maps.

1. **Report Generation**:

– Researchers can generate reports and presentations directly from MATLAB to communicate their findings effectively.

Case Studies

1. **Climate Modeling**:

– MATLAB is used for climate modeling to understand and predict climate changes, including temperature trends and sea level rise.

1. **Ecological Modeling**:

– Ecologists use MATLAB to model ecosystems, population dynamics, and species interactions.

1. **Water Resource Management**:

– MATLAB is applied in the management of water resources, including groundwater modeling, watershed analysis, and reservoir management.

1. **Environmental Impact Assessment**:

– Environmental impact assessments of construction projects, urban planning, and infrastructure development often involve MATLAB simulations and analysis.

IN SUMMARY, MATLAB serves as a valuable tool in environmental science modeling due to its capabilities in data analysis, mathematical modeling, and visualization. Environmental scientists and researchers leverage MATLAB to better understand the Earth's environment, predict future changes, and make informed decisions regarding environmental management and conservation. Its versatility and integration with GIS and remote sensing data make it an essential tool for addressing environmental challenges.

Chapter 9: MATLAB for Engineers

9.1. Electrical Engineering Applications

IN THE REALM OF ELECTRICAL engineering, MATLAB is an indispensable tool that empowers engineers to design, analyze, and simulate complex electrical systems and circuits. This section explores various applications of MATLAB in electrical engineering, showcasing how it enhances the efficiency and effectiveness of engineering tasks.

Circuit Analysis and Design

1. **Circuit Simulation**:

– MATLAB's Simulink, a graphical simulation tool, enables engineers to model and simulate electrical circuits, aiding in the analysis of circuit behavior under different conditions.

1. **Power Electronics**:

– MATLAB is utilized in the design and analysis of power electronic circuits, including converters, inverters, and rectifiers.

1. **Control Systems**:

– Engineers employ MATLAB for control system design, analysis, and tuning, ensuring stable and efficient control of electrical systems.

Signal Processing and Communication

1. **Signal Analysis**:

– MATLAB offers a wide range of signal processing functions and tools for engineers to analyze and manipulate signals, making it ideal for tasks such as filtering, modulation, and demodulation.

1. **Image Processing**:

– In image and video processing, MATLAB provides advanced algorithms for tasks like image enhancement, segmentation, and object recognition.

1. **Communication Systems**:

– Engineers design and simulate communication systems using MATLAB, evaluating parameters like modulation schemes, channel modeling, and error correction coding.

Electrical Machine Analysis

1. **Motor Control**:

– MATLAB is employed in motor control applications, enabling engineers to design controllers for motors, analyze performance, and implement control algorithms.

1. **Transformer Design**:

– Engineers use MATLAB to optimize transformer design, taking into account parameters like core material, winding arrangement, and efficiency.

Power Systems Analysis

1. **Power Flow Analysis**:

– MATLAB is utilized for power flow analysis, helping engineers assess the steady-state operation of electrical power systems.

1. **Fault Analysis**:

– Engineers simulate fault conditions in power systems to evaluate protection schemes and assess the impact of faults on system components.

Renewable Energy Systems

1. **Solar PV System Modeling**:

– MATLAB aids in modeling and simulating photovoltaic (PV) systems, optimizing the placement and sizing of solar panels for maximum energy production.

1. **Wind Energy Modeling**:

– Engineers use MATLAB to model wind turbines and analyze wind energy potential at specific locations.

Hardware-in-the-Loop (HIL) Testing

1. **Real-Time Simulation**:

– MATLAB and Simulink support HIL testing, allowing engineers to test control algorithms in real-time with physical hardware.

Robotics and Automation

1. **Robot Control**:

   – Engineers utilize MATLAB for robot control and kinematics, enabling precise motion control and trajectory planning.

1. **Automation Systems**:

   – MATLAB is applied in the design and optimization of automation systems, ensuring efficient and reliable manufacturing processes.

Electromagnetic Analysis

1. **Antenna Design**:

   – MATLAB is used for antenna design and analysis, optimizing antenna parameters for improved performance.

1. **Electromagnetic Compatibility (EMC)**:

   – Engineers assess EMC in electronic devices and circuits, identifying and mitigating electromagnetic interference using MATLAB simulations.

IN SUMMARY, MATLAB serves as a versatile and powerful tool for electrical engineers, facilitating circuit design, signal processing, control systems analysis, and more. Its broad range of applications makes it a go-to platform for solving complex electrical engineering challenges, contributing to innovation and advancement in the field. Whether designing renewable energy systems or analyzing control algorithms, MATLAB is an invaluable resource for electrical engineers worldwide.

9.2. Mechanical Engineering Simulations

MECHANICAL ENGINEERING relies heavily on simulations to design and analyze various mechanical systems, structures, and components. MATLAB is a powerful tool for mechanical engineers, offering a wide range of capabilities for simulation, modeling, and analysis in this field.

Finite Element Analysis (FEA)

FINITE ELEMENT ANALYSIS (FEA) is a fundamental technique in mechanical engineering for assessing the structural integrity and behavior of complex systems. MATLAB, combined with toolboxes like the Partial Differential Equation Toolbox, enables engineers to perform FEA with ease. Engineers can create finite element models, solve linear and nonlinear structural problems, and visualize results efficiently.

Here's an example of how MATLAB can be used for FEA:

```
% Define the geometry and mesh

model = createpde();

geometryFromEdges(model, 'LShape.stl');

mesh = generateMesh(model);

% Define material properties and boundary conditions

E = 210e9; % Young's modulus (Pa)

nu = 0.3; % Poisson's ratio
```

```
structuralProperties(model, 'YoungsModulus', E, 'PoissonsRatio', nu);

% Apply boundary conditions and loads

structuralBC(model, 'Edge', 1, 'Constraint', 'fixed');

structuralBC(model, 'Edge', 2, 'Constraint', 'fixed');

structuralBC(model, 'Edge', 4, 'Constraint', 'fixed');

structuralBoundaryLoad(model, 'Edge', 3, 'SurfaceTraction', [0; -1e5; 0]);

% Solve the structural problem

results = solve(model);

% Visualize the results

pdeplot3D(model, 'ColorMapData', results.Displacement.uz)
```

Multibody Dynamics

MECHANICAL SYSTEMS with multiple interconnected bodies require dynamic analysis to understand their behavior. MATLAB, along with the Simscape Multibody toolbox, provides a platform for modeling and simulating multibody dynamics systems. Engineers can create 3D mechanical models, define constraints, and simulate complex interactions.

```
% Create a multibody system

model = simscape.multibody.Model;

body1 = addBody(model, 'Body', 'name', 'Chassis');

body2 = addBody(model, 'Body', 'name', 'Wheel1');
```

```
body3 = addBody(model, 'Body', 'name', 'Wheel2');

% Define joints and connections

joint1 = addJoint(model, 'Revolute', 'name', 'Joint1');

joint2 = addJoint(model, 'Revolute', 'name', 'Joint2');

connectBodies(model, 'Chassis', 'Wheel1', joint1);

connectBodies(model, 'Chassis', 'Wheel2', joint2);

% Specify motion and parameters

motion1 = setMotion(joint1, 'Position', 'theta1(t)');

motion2 = setMotion(joint2, 'Position', 'theta2(t)');

body1.Mass = 10;

body2.Mass = 2;

body3.Mass = 2;

% Simulate the multibody system

simOut = sim(model);

% Analyze and visualize simulation results

plot(simOut)
```

Structural Analysis and Design

MATLAB OFFERS A WIDE array of tools for structural analysis and design, making it invaluable for mechanical engineers. Whether it's analyzing stresses in a bridge or optimizing the shape of a mechanical component, MATLAB provides the necessary functionalities. Engineers can perform tasks like linear and nonlinear static analysis, modal analysis, and shape optimization.

Here's a simple example of structural analysis:

```
% Define a truss structure

nodes = [0, 0; 4, 0; 2, 3; 6, 3];

elements = [1, 2; 1, 3; 2, 3; 2, 4; 3, 4];

elementLengths = sqrt(diff(nodes(elements), 1, 2).^2 * [1; 1]);

% Define material properties

E = 70e9; % Young's modulus (Pa)

A = 0.01; % Cross-sectional area (m^2)

% Assemble stiffness matrix

K = zeros(8, 8);

for i = 1:size(elements, 1)

n1 = elements(i, 1);

n2 = elements(i, 2);

L = elementLengths(i);

k = (E * A / L) * [1, -1; -1, 1];

% Add contributions to global stiffness matrix

K([2 * n1 - 1, 2 * n1, 2 * n2 - 1, 2 * n2], ...

[2 * n1 - 1, 2 * n1, 2 * n2 - 1, 2 * n2]) = ...

K([2 * n1 - 1, 2 * n1, 2 * n2 - 1, 2 * n2], ...
```

```
[2 * n1 - 1, 2 * n1, 2 * n2 - 1, 2 * n2]) + k;

end

% Apply boundary conditions and loads

u = zeros(8, 1); % Displacement vector

F = zeros(8, 1); % Force vector

u([1, 2, 5, 6]) = [0; 0; 0; 0]; % Fixed nodes

F([3, 4, 7, 8]) = [0; 0; -1000; 0]; % Applied load

% Solve for displacements

displacements = K \ F;

% Calculate stresses and strains

stresses = zeros(size(elements, 1), 1);

strains = zeros(size(elements, 1), 1);

for i = 1:size(elements, 1)

n1 = elements(i, 1);

n2 = elements(i, 2);

L
```

9.3. Civil Engineering and MATLAB

CIVIL ENGINEERING INVOLVES the design, construction, and maintenance of infrastructure and large-scale systems, including bridges, buildings, roads, and dams. MATLAB serves as a versatile platform for civil engineers, offering tools and capabilities to address various aspects of civil engineering projects.

Structural Analysis and Design

STRUCTURAL ANALYSIS and design are fundamental in civil engineering to ensure the safety and stability of structures. MATLAB provides a wide range of functions and toolboxes for structural engineers to perform tasks such as finite element analysis (FEA), structural dynamics analysis, and concrete and steel design.

For instance, MATLAB's Structural Analysis Toolbox allows engineers to model complex structural systems, apply loads and constraints, and analyze deflections, stresses, and modal responses. Additionally, MATLAB can automate the design of concrete and steel structures based on local building codes and design standards.

Geotechnical Engineering

GEOTECHNICAL ENGINEERING deals with soil mechanics and the behavior of soil and rock materials in engineering applications. MATLAB can be used to analyze geotechnical data, perform soil stability and settlement calculations, and model the behavior of foundations and retaining walls.

Engineers can create MATLAB scripts to analyze the results of soil tests, generate soil profiles, and calculate bearing capacities. MATLAB's capabilities in data visualization and analysis are particularly useful in geotechnical engineering projects, where large datasets need to be processed and interpreted.

Transportation Engineering

TRANSPORTATION ENGINEERS focus on the planning, design, and operation of transportation systems, including highways, railways, airports, and traffic management. MATLAB can aid in traffic flow modeling, optimization of transportation networks, and analysis of vehicle and pedestrian behavior.

With MATLAB, engineers can simulate traffic scenarios, evaluate congestion and traffic flow patterns, and optimize signal timings at intersections. This enables the efficient design of transportation systems that reduce congestion, improve safety, and enhance overall transportation infrastructure.

Environmental Engineering

ENVIRONMENTAL ENGINEERS address environmental issues related to water quality, air pollution, waste management, and sustainable practices. MATLAB is used in environmental engineering to model environmental processes, analyze pollution data, and design pollution control systems.

Engineers can create MATLAB scripts to model water quality in rivers and lakes, predict air pollutant dispersion, and optimize wastewater treatment processes. MATLAB's mathematical modeling capabilities are crucial in understanding and mitigating environmental challenges.

Project Management and Optimization

CIVIL ENGINEERING PROJECTS often involve complex logistics, resource allocation, and project scheduling. MATLAB can be used to develop optimization models for project management, resource allocation, and cost estimation.

Engineers can create MATLAB algorithms to optimize construction schedules, allocate resources efficiently, and minimize project costs.

This helps civil engineers streamline project management and ensure the timely completion of infrastructure projects.

In summary, MATLAB plays a significant role in civil engineering by providing a powerful platform for structural analysis, geotechnical engineering, transportation planning, environmental analysis, and project management. Its versatility and extensive toolbox ecosystem make it an indispensable tool for civil engineers working on a wide range of infrastructure projects.

9.4. Aerospace Engineering: Modeling and Analysis

AEROSPACE ENGINEERING involves the design, development, and analysis of aircraft, spacecraft, and related systems. MATLAB is a versatile tool extensively used in aerospace engineering for various purposes, from modeling and simulation to data analysis and control system design.

Aircraft and Spacecraft Design

MATLAB IS EMPLOYED in the initial stages of aircraft and spacecraft design to model the aerodynamics, propulsion, and structural properties of vehicles. Engineers use MATLAB to simulate flight conditions, analyze airfoil shapes, and optimize the design to achieve desired performance characteristics.

For instance, MATLAB can be used to create aerodynamic models that simulate airflow around an aircraft's wings and predict lift and drag forces. These simulations aid in designing efficient and stable aircraft configurations.

Flight Dynamics and Control

IN AEROSPACE ENGINEERING, flight dynamics and control are critical aspects of ensuring the stability and maneuverability of aircraft and spacecraft. MATLAB offers tools for modeling the dynamic behavior of vehicles, developing control algorithms, and simulating flight scenarios.

Engineers can use MATLAB to design control systems that stabilize aircraft or spacecraft, control propulsion systems, and optimize trajectories. The Simulink toolbox, integrated with MATLAB, allows engineers to create detailed flight simulations with real-time control.

Orbital Mechanics and Space Missions

AEROSPACE ENGINEERS rely on MATLAB for orbital mechanics calculations and mission planning. MATLAB's computational capabilities are used to predict and analyze the motion of objects in space, calculate orbits, and plan trajectories for space missions.

For instance, MATLAB can be used to determine launch windows for interplanetary missions, calculate transfer orbits between celestial bodies, and perform orbital rendezvous simulations. These calculations are essential for the successful execution of space missions.

Structural Analysis and Materials

THE STRUCTURAL INTEGRITY of aerospace vehicles is crucial for ensuring their safety and reliability. MATLAB is used for structural analysis, including finite element analysis (FEA) and stress analysis. Engineers can assess the performance of materials under extreme conditions and optimize structural designs.

MATLAB also aids in the selection of materials based on their mechanical properties, thermal conductivity, and weight considerations. This ensures that aerospace vehicles are constructed with materials that can withstand the harsh conditions of space or high-speed flight.

Propulsion Systems and Rocketry

PROPULSION SYSTEMS are at the heart of aerospace engineering, and MATLAB is instrumental in their analysis and design. Engineers can use MATLAB to model and simulate propulsion systems, calculate thrust profiles, and optimize engine performance.

MATLAB's capabilities are applied to rocketry, including trajectory analysis, stage separation simulations, and engine performance optimization. This is crucial for the development of launch vehicles and spacecraft propulsion systems.

In summary, MATLAB plays a significant role in aerospace engineering by providing a comprehensive platform for aircraft and spacecraft design, flight dynamics and control, orbital mechanics, structural analysis, materials selection, and propulsion system analysis. Its versatility and extensive toolbox ecosystem make it an indispensable tool for aerospace engineers working on the development and analysis of aerospace vehicles and systems.

9.5. Automotive Engineering: Modeling and Analysis

AUTOMOTIVE ENGINEERING is a multidisciplinary field that focuses on the design, development, and analysis of automobiles and their subsystems. MATLAB serves as a valuable tool in automotive engineering, offering capabilities for modeling, simulation, control system design, and data analysis.

Vehicle Dynamics and Handling

ONE OF THE PRIMARY areas where MATLAB is used in automotive engineering is vehicle dynamics and handling analysis. Engineers employ MATLAB to model the dynamic behavior of vehicles under different driving conditions, including steering, braking, and acceleration.

Using MATLAB's Simulink toolbox, engineers can create comprehensive vehicle dynamics models that simulate how a vehicle responds to driver inputs and road conditions. This allows for the optimization of vehicle handling characteristics, such as stability, ride comfort, and safety.

Powertrain and Engine Simulation

MATLAB IS EXTENSIVELY used to model and simulate powertrains and engines in automobiles. Engineers can create detailed models of internal combustion engines, electric motors, and hybrid powertrains to evaluate their performance and efficiency.

Simulation in MATLAB allows engineers to optimize engine parameters, control strategies, and transmission systems. This aids in the development of fuel-efficient and environmentally friendly vehicles.

Control System Design

CONTROL SYSTEMS ARE vital in modern automobiles to ensure safe and efficient operation. MATLAB offers a platform for designing and simulating control systems for various vehicle subsystems, including engine control, anti-lock braking systems (ABS), and stability control.

Engineers can use MATLAB to develop control algorithms, perform real-time simulations, and validate their designs before implementation. This results in improved vehicle safety, performance, and fuel efficiency.

Autonomous and Connected Vehicles

THE AUTOMOTIVE INDUSTRY is increasingly focused on autonomous and connected vehicles. MATLAB plays a crucial role in the development of these technologies. Engineers can use MATLAB to create sensor fusion algorithms for autonomous vehicles, enabling them to perceive their surroundings accurately.

Additionally, MATLAB facilitates the simulation of vehicle-to-vehicle (V2V) and vehicle-to-infrastructure (V2I) communication systems, essential for connected vehicles. These simulations help in optimizing communication protocols and evaluating the impact on traffic flow and safety.

Noise, Vibration, and Harshness (NVH) Analysis

TO ENHANCE PASSENGER comfort and vehicle quality, automotive engineers use MATLAB for noise, vibration, and harshness (NVH) analysis. MATLAB enables the modeling and simulation of NVH effects, allowing engineers to identify and mitigate sources of noise and vibration in vehicles.

By analyzing the NVH characteristics of various vehicle components and systems, engineers can make design improvements that result in quieter and more comfortable vehicles.

Data Analysis and Testing

MATLAB IS A VALUABLE tool for processing and analyzing data collected during vehicle testing and validation. Engineers can use MATLAB to perform statistical analysis, generate reports, and visualize test data to gain insights into vehicle performance and reliability.

Furthermore, MATLAB facilitates the development of virtual test environments, reducing the need for physical testing and accelerating the vehicle development process.

In conclusion, MATLAB plays a significant role in automotive engineering by offering capabilities in vehicle dynamics, powertrain simulation, control system design, autonomous and connected vehicles, NVH analysis, and data analysis. Its versatility and extensive toolset make it an indispensable tool for automotive engineers working on the design, development, and analysis of modern automobiles.

10.1. Writing Academic Papers with MATLAB Figures

Academic research often involves the presentation of complex data and results in a clear and visually appealing manner. MATLAB is a versatile tool that can assist researchers in generating high-quality figures and plots for inclusion in academic papers, theses, and dissertations. In this section, we will explore how MATLAB can be used effectively for creating publication-ready figures and discuss best practices for incorporating them into academic documents.

Benefits of Using MATLAB for Academic Figures

1. **Versatility**: MATLAB offers a wide range of plot types, including 2D and 3D plots, scatter plots, bar charts, histograms, and more. This versatility allows researchers to represent various types of data accurately.
2. **Customization**: MATLAB provides extensive customization options for figures, allowing researchers to tailor the appearance of plots to match the requirements of their academic papers. Customization options include fonts, colors, line styles, and axis properties.
3. **Data Analysis**: MATLAB can be used to perform data analysis and statistical calculations, making it easy to generate plots that illustrate research findings effectively.
4. **Export Options**: MATLAB allows users to export figures in various formats, such as vector graphics (e.g., PDF, EPS) or raster images (e.g., PNG, JPEG), ensuring compatibility with academic document formatting requirements.

Creating Publication-Quality Figures in MATLAB

WHEN CREATING FIGURES for academic papers, researchers should follow these best practices:

1. **Choose the Right Plot Type**: Select a plot type that best represents the data and the message you want to convey. Common types include line plots for trends, bar charts for comparisons, and scatter plots for correlations.
2. **Label Axes and Legends**: Clearly label the x and y-axes of your plots, and include legends when multiple datasets are plotted. Use descriptive labels and units.
3. **Use Appropriate Colors**: Ensure that colors are distinguishable and consider using color palettes that are accessible to all readers, including those with color vision deficiencies.
4. **Adjust Fonts and Sizes**: Use legible fonts and appropriate font sizes for text on the plot, including axis labels, titles, and legends. Aim for consistency in font usage throughout your document.
5. **Control Line Styles and Marker Types**: Customize line styles (e.g., solid, dashed) and marker types (e.g., circles, squares) to make your plots visually appealing and easy to understand.
6. **Handle Missing Data**: Handle missing or incomplete data appropriately, and clearly indicate gaps in your plots to maintain data integrity.
7. **Export in High-Quality Formats**: Export your figures in high-resolution formats suitable for publication. Vector formats like PDF and EPS are preferred for maintaining image quality.

Including MATLAB Figures in Academic Documents

ONCE YOU HAVE CREATED publication-quality figures in MATLAB, you can incorporate them into your academic papers using the following steps:

1. Export the MATLAB figure to your desired format (e.g., PDF or EPS) using the saveas function or the export options in the MATLAB Figure window.
2. Insert the exported figure into your academic document using the document editing software of your choice (e.g., LaTeX, Microsoft Word). Ensure that the figure retains its quality and readability.
3. Reference the figure in your document's caption or text, providing a clear explanation of the figure's content and its relevance to your research.

By following these guidelines, researchers can effectively utilize MATLAB to create informative and visually appealing figures for their academic publications, enhancing the clarity and impact of their research findings.

10.2. MATLAB in Thesis and Dissertation Research

MATLAB IS A POWERFUL tool that can greatly benefit graduate students working on their theses and dissertations. Whether your research involves data analysis, simulations, modeling, or any other computational tasks, MATLAB offers a wide range of functionalities to support your academic work. In this section, we will explore how MATLAB can be used effectively in thesis and dissertation research.

Data Analysis and Visualization

MANY RESEARCH PROJECTS involve collecting and analyzing data. MATLAB provides a robust environment for data analysis and visualization. Here's how MATLAB can assist in this aspect of your research:

1. **Data Import**: MATLAB allows you to easily import data from various file formats, such as Excel spreadsheets, CSV files, and databases. You can use functions like readtable and csvread to load your data.
2. **Data Cleaning**: MATLAB provides tools for cleaning and preprocessing data, including handling missing values, outliers, and noise. Functions like fillmissing and isoutlier can help ensure the quality of your dataset.
3. **Statistical Analysis**: MATLAB offers a comprehensive suite of statistical functions for hypothesis testing, regression analysis, and descriptive statistics. You can perform t-tests, ANOVA, and correlation analysis with ease.
4. **Data Visualization**: MATLAB's plotting capabilities allow you to create publication-quality charts and graphs to visualize your data. Functions like plot, histogram, and boxplot enable you to represent your findings effectively.

Simulation and Modeling

IF YOUR RESEARCH INVOLVES simulations or mathematical modeling, MATLAB provides a flexible platform for creating, running, and analyzing models:

1. **Simulink Integration**: MATLAB seamlessly integrates with Simulink, a powerful simulation tool. You can build dynamic system models, control systems, and perform

simulations to validate your hypotheses.

2. **Differential Equations**: MATLAB excels at solving ordinary and partial differential equations. You can use functions like ode45 and pdepe to simulate dynamic systems and physical processes.
3. **Optimization**: MATLAB's optimization toolbox offers various algorithms for solving optimization problems, which are often encountered in engineering and scientific research.

Writing and Documentation

AS YOU WORK ON YOUR thesis or dissertation, MATLAB can assist in organizing your research and generating documentation:

1. **Live Scripts**: MATLAB's Live Scripts allow you to combine code, text, and visualizations in a single document. You can use Live Scripts to create comprehensive and interactive reports for your research.
2. **LaTeX Integration**: If you're using LaTeX for your thesis or dissertation, MATLAB can generate figures and tables directly in LaTeX format. This integration streamlines the inclusion of MATLAB-generated content in your document.
3. **Version Control**: MATLAB can be integrated with version control systems like Git, enabling you to track changes and collaborate with advisors and peers more efficiently.

Collaboration and Presentation

MATLAB SUPPORTS COLLABORATION and presentation aspects of your research:

1. **Sharing Code**: You can share your MATLAB code with collaborators or advisors, making it easier to collaborate on research projects.
2. **Creating Presentations**: MATLAB's publishing capabilities allow you to create presentations and slideshows with embedded code, visualizations, and explanations.
3. **Interactive Reports**: MATLAB allows you to create interactive reports and dashboards, enhancing your ability to present your findings to a wider audience.

In summary, MATLAB is a valuable resource for graduate students working on their theses and dissertations. Its capabilities in data analysis, modeling, documentation, and collaboration can streamline the research process and enhance the quality of your academic work. Whether you are in the fields of engineering, science, or any other discipline, MATLAB can be a valuable ally in your graduate research journey.

10.3. Collaborative Research Using MATLAB

COLLABORATIVE RESEARCH is a cornerstone of scientific progress. It brings together researchers from different backgrounds and expertise to work collectively on complex problems. MATLAB offers several features and tools that facilitate collaborative research efforts, making it a preferred choice for many research projects involving multiple contributors.

Version Control with Git

GIT IS A WIDELY USED version control system that enables multiple researchers to work on the same codebase simultaneously while keeping track of changes and revisions. MATLAB seamlessly integrates with Git, allowing researchers to:

1. **Track Changes**: Researchers can commit their changes, branch off from the main project, and merge their work when it's ready, ensuring that everyone is working with up-to-date code.
2. **Collaborative Coding**: MATLAB's integration with Git enables multiple researchers to contribute to the same project without conflicts. Each researcher can create a branch to work on a specific task and merge it back into the main codebase when completed.
3. **Code Review**: Researchers can use Git to perform code reviews, where team members can provide feedback on code changes, suggest improvements, and ensure code quality.
4. **Code History**: Git maintains a detailed history of changes, making it easy to track when and why specific modifications were made. This is crucial for research reproducibility and accountability.

Sharing Code and Data

MATLAB PROVIDES VARIOUS ways to share code and data with collaborators:

1. **MATLAB Online**: MATLAB Online allows collaborators to access and work on MATLAB projects via a web browser. This eliminates the need to install MATLAB on each collaborator's computer.
2. **MATLAB Drive**: MATLAB Drive provides cloud storage for MATLAB files and data, making it easy to share code, data, and results with team members. It ensures that

everyone has access to the most current project materials.

3. **MAT Files**: MATLAB's native data format, MAT files, can store variables, data, and models. Collaborators can exchange MAT files to share data, results, or trained machine learning models.

Simulink Collaboration

FOR COLLABORATIVE RESEARCH involving simulations and modeling with Simulink, MATLAB offers features such as:

1. **Simulink Projects**: Simulink projects allow researchers to organize their Simulink models, scripts, and data in a structured manner. Collaborators can work within the same project, ensuring that all related components are kept together.
2. **Model Referencing**: Simulink supports model referencing, allowing researchers to create modular and reusable Simulink models. This makes it easier to collaborate on complex systems by breaking them down into manageable components.

Real-Time Collaboration

MATLAB SUPPORTS REAL-time collaboration, enabling researchers to work together seamlessly:

1. **Live Editor**: MATLAB's Live Editor allows multiple researchers to work on the same script or document simultaneously. This real-time collaboration is especially helpful when researchers need to write code, generate visualizations, or prepare reports together.
2. **MATLAB Online Sharing**: Researchers can share MATLAB Online sessions with colleagues, providing

them with direct access to MATLAB environments, code, and data.

3. **Live Apps**: MATLAB allows researchers to create interactive live apps that can be shared with collaborators. These apps can include user interfaces and visualizations, making it easy for collaborators to interact with research tools.

In conclusion, MATLAB's robust support for version control, code sharing, Simulink collaboration, and real-time cooperation makes it an ideal platform for collaborative research projects. Whether working on large-scale simulations, data analysis, or machine learning projects, MATLAB's collaborative features enhance productivity and facilitate successful teamwork in research endeavors.

10.4. Data Management and Archiving

EFFECTIVE DATA MANAGEMENT is a critical aspect of research, ensuring that data is organized, preserved, and easily accessible for future reference. In the context of MATLAB, managing and archiving data involves several strategies and best practices.

Organizing Data

PROPERLY ORGANIZING your research data is the foundation of effective data management. MATLAB provides tools and conventions to structure your data efficiently:

1. **Folder Structure**: Create a well-structured folder hierarchy to store your MATLAB scripts, data files, and other project-related materials. Organizing files into

folders based on their purpose or data type helps keep everything organized and easily navigable.

2. **MAT Files**: Use MAT files to save and load variables and datasets. By storing data in MAT files, you ensure that it can be easily accessed and shared with collaborators or future researchers.
3. **Script and Function Naming**: Adopt consistent naming conventions for your MATLAB scripts and functions. This practice makes it easier to locate and understand your code.
4. **Documentation**: Include comprehensive documentation for your data and code. Use comments in your MATLAB scripts to describe the purpose of functions, variables, and the data they manipulate. Proper documentation ensures that you and others can understand and use your work in the future.

Version Control for Data

JUST AS VERSION CONTROL is essential for code, it's equally important for data management. Git, as mentioned in the previous section, can be used not only for code but also for tracking changes in data files. This provides a clear history of data modifications, making it easier to reproduce research results and collaborate effectively.

Data Archiving

DATA ARCHIVING ENSURES the long-term preservation of your research data. It's important to follow best practices for archiving, which include:

1. **Data Repositories**: Consider depositing your research data in specialized data repositories or archives relevant to your field. Many research institutions and organizations

provide data repositories for this purpose.

2. **Metadata**: Create metadata files that provide detailed information about your data, including data format, variables, units, and any relevant context. Metadata is crucial for understanding and reusing data in the future.
3. **Data Formats**: Choose standardized data formats that are widely accepted in your field. This ensures that your data can be read and used by other researchers and software tools.
4. **Backup and Redundancy**: Maintain backups of your data in multiple locations to prevent data loss due to hardware failures or other unforeseen events.
5. **Data Access Policy**: Clearly define who can access your archived data and under what conditions. Some data may need to be embargoed for a period before becoming publicly available.

Data Licensing

CONSIDER THE LICENSING of your data when archiving it. Licensing defines how others can use, share, and build upon your data. Choose a license that aligns with your preferences and the goals of your research. Common data licenses include open access licenses and more restrictive licenses that control data usage.

Data Privacy and Ethics

WHEN ARCHIVING RESEARCH data, ensure that you comply with data privacy regulations and ethical considerations. Anonymize or de-identify sensitive data to protect privacy, and obtain appropriate permissions when necessary.

In summary, effective data management and archiving practices are essential for preserving the integrity and accessibility of your research data. MATLAB provides tools and integration with version control systems like Git to help streamline these processes. By following best practices for data organization, version control, archiving, and licensing, you contribute to the reproducibility and transparency of your research, benefiting both current and future scientific endeavors.

10.5. Ethical Considerations in Computational Research

ETHICAL CONSIDERATIONS are paramount in computational research, including the use of MATLAB. Ensuring ethical practices not only upholds the integrity of your work but also contributes to responsible research and innovation. In this section, we explore some key ethical considerations that researchers using MATLAB should be aware of.

1. Data Privacy and Security

PROTECTING THE PRIVACY and security of data is a fundamental ethical responsibility. When working with sensitive data in MATLAB, consider the following:

- **Data Anonymization**: If your research involves personal or sensitive data, anonymize or de-identify the data to protect individuals' privacy.
- **Data Encryption**: Implement encryption mechanisms when handling confidential data to prevent unauthorized access.
- **Secure Storage**: Store sensitive data in secure locations with access controls to limit who can view or modify it.

2. Research Integrity

MAINTAINING RESEARCH integrity is crucial to building trust in the scientific community. Ethical considerations related to research integrity in MATLAB include:

- **Reproducibility**: Ensure that your MATLAB code and data are well-documented and accessible to others for validation and reproducibility.

- **Honesty**: Be honest about your contributions and potential conflicts of interest in your research.

- **Citing Sources**: Properly attribute the work of others by citing relevant sources and acknowledging their contributions.

3. Responsible AI and Machine Learning

WHEN DEVELOPING AI and machine learning models in MATLAB, consider ethical AI principles:

- **Bias Mitigation**: Take steps to identify and mitigate biases in your data and models to ensure fairness.

- **Transparency**: Make your AI models transparent and interpretable, allowing users to understand how decisions are made.

- **Accountability**: Implement mechanisms to trace the decisions made by AI systems back to their sources.

4. Inclusivity and Accessibility

ENSURE THAT YOUR RESEARCH is inclusive and accessible to a diverse audience:

- **Accessibility**: Design MATLAB interfaces and visualizations with accessibility features to accommodate users with disabilities.

- **Diversity and Inclusion**: Promote diversity and inclusion in your research team and consider the potential impacts of your work on different groups.

5. Ethical Use of MATLAB Toolboxes

IF YOUR RESEARCH INVOLVES specialized toolboxes in MATLAB, be aware of any ethical considerations specific to those domains. For example:

- **Medical Ethics**: When using MATLAB for medical research, adhere to medical ethics guidelines, including patient consent and confidentiality.

- **Environmental Impact**: Consider the environmental impact of your research, especially when running computationally intensive simulations.

6. Collaboration and Attribution

IN COLLABORATIVE RESEARCH involving MATLAB, establish clear guidelines for authorship, data sharing, and the use of code. Provide proper attribution to collaborators and acknowledge their contributions.

7. Compliance with Regulations

DEPENDING ON YOUR RESEARCH area, you may need to comply with specific regulations and ethical guidelines set by institutions or governing bodies. Ensure that your MATLAB-based research adheres to these regulations.

8. Ethics Review

FOR RESEARCH INVOLVING human subjects, animals, or other sensitive areas, seek ethical review and approval from relevant ethics committees or boards.

In conclusion, ethical considerations should be an integral part of your MATLAB-based research. Upholding ethical standards not only safeguards the credibility of your work but also contributes to the responsible advancement of science and technology. Always stay informed about ethical guidelines and seek guidance from ethics experts or committees when necessary. By doing so, you can conduct research that benefits society while respecting ethical principles.

Chapter 11: Scripting and Automation

Section 11.1: Automating Repetitive Tasks

IN MATLAB, AUTOMATING repetitive tasks is a powerful capability that can save you significant time and effort. Whether it's processing large datasets, performing simulations, or executing a sequence of commands, MATLAB provides various tools and techniques for scripting and automation. In this section, we'll explore how to create scripts, functions, and utilize control structures to automate tasks efficiently.

Writing MATLAB Scripts

ONE OF THE FUNDAMENTAL ways to automate tasks in MATLAB is by creating scripts. A script is a plain text file with a .m extension that contains a series of MATLAB commands. When you run a script, MATLAB executes the commands sequentially. Here's a simple example:

```
% Example MATLAB Script

x = 1:10;

y = x.^2;

plot(x, y);

xlabel('x');

ylabel('y');

title('Plot of y = x^2');
```

To run the script, you can simply type its filename (without the .m extension) in the MATLAB command window, and MATLAB will execute all the commands in the script.

Defining MATLAB Functions

WHILE SCRIPTS ARE USEFUL for a series of commands, functions offer more flexibility and reusability. Functions allow you to encapsulate a set of commands into a named block, making it easy to call and reuse. Here's an example of a simple MATLAB function:

```
% Example MATLAB Function

function result = square(x)

result = x^2;

end
```

You can save this function in a separate .m file and then call it from the MATLAB command window or from other scripts and functions.

Control Structures for Automation

MATLAB PROVIDES VARIOUS control structures that enable automation based on conditions and iterations. These include if statements for conditional execution and for and while loops for repeated execution.

Here's an example of using a for loop to compute the sum of the first 10 natural numbers:

```
% Using a for loop for automation

sum = 0;
```

```
for i = 1:10

sum = sum + i;

end

disp(['Sum of first 10 natural numbers: ' num2str(sum)]);
```

This loop iterates from 1 to 10 and accumulates the sum. The disp function is used to display the result.

Automation in MATLAB Projects

IN MORE COMPLEX SCENARIOS, automation becomes crucial in MATLAB projects. You might need to process large datasets, perform simulations, or run optimization routines. MATLAB provides tools like the MATLAB Editor and Live Editor, which support script development, debugging, and documentation.

Additionally, you can utilize the MATLAB Command Window to execute single commands interactively, which is often handy for quick tests and exploratory work.

In summary, MATLAB offers powerful capabilities for automating repetitive tasks, whether through scripts, functions, or control structures. By leveraging these features, you can enhance your productivity and streamline your workflows in MATLAB.

Section 11.2: Building Custom Functions

CUSTOM FUNCTIONS IN MATLAB are an essential tool for automating tasks, encapsulating functionality, and promoting code reusability. In this section, we'll explore the creation of custom functions, including input/output arguments, local variables, and best practices.

Defining Custom Functions

A CUSTOM FUNCTION IN MATLAB is a separate .m file containing a set of commands that perform a specific task or computation. Custom functions can have input arguments (parameters) and output arguments (return values). Here's a simple example of a custom function that computes the factorial of a number:

```
% Custom function to calculate factorial

function result = factorial(n)

result = 1;

for i = 1:n

result = result * i;

end

end
```

This function accepts one input argument n, which represents the number whose factorial we want to calculate. It returns the result as an output argument.

Input and Output Arguments

INPUT ARGUMENTS ALLOW you to pass values into a function, making it more flexible. Output arguments enable the function to return results to the calling code. MATLAB functions can have multiple input and output arguments, as needed for the task at hand.

```
% Custom function with multiple input and output arguments
```

```
function [sum_result, product_result] = calculate_sum_and_product(a, b)

sum_result = a + b;

product_result = a * b;

end
```

In this example, the function calculate_sum_and_product takes two input arguments (a and b) and returns two output arguments (sum_result and product_result).

Local Variables

LOCAL VARIABLES ARE variables defined within a function and are accessible only within that function's scope. They do not interfere with variables outside the function, helping to avoid naming conflicts. It's good practice to use local variables when necessary to isolate the function's logic.

```
% Using local variables in a custom function

function result = compute_average(numbers)

sum_numbers = sum(numbers);

count = length(numbers);

result = sum_numbers / count;

end
```

In this function, sum_numbers and count are local variables used to perform the calculation of the average.

Best Practices

WHEN CREATING CUSTOM functions in MATLAB, consider the following best practices:

1. Use clear and descriptive function names.
2. Document your functions with comments to explain their purpose and usage.
3. Include error checking and handling to make your functions robust.
4. Organize your code logically within functions to improve readability.
5. Test your functions thoroughly to ensure they produce the expected results.

By following these best practices, you can create well-structured and reliable custom functions that enhance automation and code maintainability in MATLAB.

Section 11.3: Batch Processing with MATLAB

BATCH PROCESSING IS a technique commonly used in MATLAB to automate the execution of a sequence of tasks or functions on multiple datasets or input parameters. It is particularly useful when you need to perform repetitive operations on a large set of data or run simulations with different configurations. In this section, we will explore the concept of batch processing in MATLAB and how to effectively implement it.

Understanding Batch Processing

BATCH PROCESSING INVOLVES running a series of MATLAB scripts or functions, often with varying input parameters, without manual intervention. It helps streamline workflows, improve productivity, and ensures consistency in data processing.

In MATLAB, batch processing can be applied to a wide range of tasks, such as data analysis, simulations, optimization, and more. Let's look at an example of a batch processing scenario where we want to analyze multiple datasets stored in separate files.

Example: Batch Processing Data Files

SUPPOSE YOU HAVE A set of data files named data1.mat, data2.mat, data3.mat, and so on, each containing measurement data. You want to perform the same data analysis operation on all these files without manually loading and processing each one.

```
% Batch processing example

dataFiles = dir('data*.mat'); % List of data files

results = cell(1, numel(dataFiles)); % Initialize results cell array

for i = 1:numel(dataFiles)

% Load data from the file

data = load(dataFiles(i).name);

% Perform data analysis or processing here

% Replace the following line with your custom analysis function

results{i} = analyzeData(data);

end
```

In this example, we use dir to list all data files matching the pattern 'data*.mat'. We then loop through each file, load its data, and perform the desired analysis or processing. The results are stored in a cell array for further examination or storage.

Custom Analysis Function

IT'S COMMON TO CREATE a custom function for the specific analysis or processing task you want to perform during batch processing. The analyzeData function in the example above represents this custom analysis function. You can define it according to your data analysis requirements.

Batch Processing Advantages

BATCH PROCESSING OFFERS several advantages in MATLAB:

1. **Efficiency**: It saves time by automating repetitive tasks.
2. **Consistency**: Ensures consistent processing across multiple datasets.
3. **Parallelization**: You can parallelize batch processing for faster execution on multi-core processors.
4. **Reproducibility**: Results are reproducible since the same processing steps are applied consistently.

By leveraging batch processing in MATLAB, you can efficiently handle large datasets, conduct parameter sweeps, or execute simulations with ease, enhancing your productivity and data analysis capabilities.

Section 11.4: Scheduler and Time-Based Operations

IN MATLAB, YOU CAN schedule and automate tasks to run at specific times or intervals using the built-in functionality for time-based operations. This capability is valuable for various applications, including data logging, system monitoring, and periodic data processing. In this section, we will explore how to create schedules and perform time-based operations in MATLAB.

Timer Objects

MATLAB PROVIDES TIMER objects to schedule and execute tasks at specified intervals. You can create timer objects, configure their properties, and define callback functions that are executed when the timer triggers.

Here's an example of how to create a simple timer object that prints a message every 2 seconds:

```
% Create a timer object

t = timer;

t.TimerFcn = @(~,~) disp('Timer triggered.');

% Set the timer interval (2 seconds)

t.Period = 2;

% Set the number of repetitions (0 for infinite)

t.ExecutionMode = 'fixedRate';

t.TasksToExecute = inf;

% Start the timer

start(t);
```

In this example, we create a timer object t and set its properties, including the timer function (TimerFcn) that displays a message when triggered, the interval (Period) of 2 seconds, and the number of repetitions (TasksToExecute) set to infinite. The timer is started using start(t).

Scheduled Tasks

YOU CAN USE TIMER OBJECTS to schedule a wide range of tasks, such as data acquisition, automated testing, or periodic updates of simulation results. Callback functions can be customized to perform specific actions when the timer triggers, making it a versatile tool for automation.

Real-Time Data Acquisition

ONE COMMON USE OF TIMERS in MATLAB is for real-time data acquisition. You can configure a timer to collect data from sensors or instruments at regular intervals, enabling continuous monitoring and data logging.

```
% Example: Real-time data acquisition

sensor = MySensorObject; % Replace with your sensor object

t = timer('TimerFcn', @(~,~) logData(sensor), 'Period', 5);

t.ExecutionMode = 'fixedRate';

t.TasksToExecute = inf;

start(t);
```

In this example, a custom logData function is called by the timer to log data from a sensor every 5 seconds.

Task Scheduling

BESIDES PERIODIC TASKS, you can also schedule tasks to run at specific times of the day or week using MATLAB's task scheduling capabilities. This is particularly useful for automated data analysis, report generation, or system maintenance.

Task Scheduler Toolbox

MATLAB ALSO PROVIDES the Task Scheduler Toolbox for more advanced task scheduling and automation, allowing you to create, manage, and schedule tasks with greater flexibility. This toolbox extends MATLAB's capabilities for batch processing and automation, especially for complex scheduling requirements.

In summary, MATLAB's timer objects and task scheduling options empower you to automate tasks and operations based on time intervals or specific schedules, enhancing your ability to manage repetitive or time-sensitive activities efficiently.

Section 11.5: Interfacing with Databases

MATLAB PROVIDES ROBUST capabilities for interfacing with databases, making it a powerful tool for data analysis and automation when dealing with structured data stored in database systems. In this section, we will explore how to connect to databases, retrieve data, perform queries, and update database records using MATLAB.

Database Connectivity

MATLAB OFFERS SUPPORT for various database management systems (DBMS) such as MySQL, PostgreSQL, Microsoft SQL Server, and more. You can establish a connection to a database using the Database Toolbox, which provides functions and classes for database interaction.

Here's a simple example of connecting to a MySQL database:

```
% Define database connection parameters

dbDriver = 'com.mysql.jdbc.Driver';

dbURL = 'jdbc:mysql://localhost/mydatabase';

dbUsername = 'yourusername';

dbPassword = 'yourpassword';

% Create a database connection

conn = database('mydatabase', dbUsername, dbPassword, dbDriver,
dbURL);
```

In this example, you specify the database driver, URL, username, and password to create a database connection object (conn) for a MySQL database.

Querying the Database

ONCE CONNECTED, YOU can execute SQL queries to retrieve data from the database. MATLAB allows you to execute simple queries, aggregate data, and fetch results into MATLAB variables for further analysis.

```
% Execute a simple SQL query

query = 'SELECT * FROM mytable WHERE column1 > 100';

result = fetch(conn, query);
```

In this code snippet, we execute a SQL query that retrieves rows from the mytable where column1 is greater than 100 and store the result in the result variable.

Updating Database Records

MATLAB ALSO ENABLES you to modify database records by executing SQL UPDATE or INSERT statements.

```
% Update records in the database

updateQuery = 'UPDATE mytable SET column2 = 42 WHERE column1 = 101';

exec(conn, updateQuery);

% Insert new records

insertQuery = 'INSERT INTO mytable (column1, column2) VALUES (102, 73)';

exec(conn, insertQuery);
```

In this example, we update a record in the database by setting column2 to 42 where column1 is equal to 101. We also insert a new record into the mytable.

Error Handling

WHEN WORKING WITH DATABASES, it's essential to handle errors gracefully. MATLAB's Database Toolbox provides error-handling mechanisms to manage exceptions that may occur during database operations.

Closing the Database Connection

AFTER COMPLETING YOUR database operations, it's good practice to close the database connection to release resources.

% Close the database connection

close(conn);

Closing the connection ensures that you free up resources and maintain a clean execution environment.

In summary, MATLAB's capabilities for interfacing with databases allow you to efficiently retrieve, analyze, and update structured data. Whether you're working with research data, business records, or any other structured dataset, MATLAB's database connectivity options make it a valuable tool for automating data-related tasks and performing advanced analyses.

Chapter 12: MATLAB for Business and Finance

Section 12.1: Analyzing Financial Markets

MATLAB IS A POWERFUL tool for analyzing financial markets and making informed investment decisions. In this section, we'll explore how MATLAB can be used in financial analysis, from data retrieval to building and backtesting trading strategies.

Data Retrieval

TO PERFORM FINANCIAL analysis, you need access to historical and real-time financial data. MATLAB offers several methods to retrieve financial data from various sources, including online databases and APIs.

```
% Retrieve historical stock data from Yahoo Finance

ticker = 'AAPL';

startDate = '01-01-2010';

endDate = '12-31-2020';

data = get_yahoo_data(ticker, startDate, endDate);
```

In this example, we use the get_yahoo_data function to fetch historical stock data for Apple Inc. from Yahoo Finance.

Data Visualization

VISUALIZING FINANCIAL data is crucial for spotting trends and patterns. MATLAB provides powerful plotting capabilities to create various financial charts, such as candlestick charts, moving averages, and more.

% Create a candlestick chart

candle(data.High, data.Low, data.Close, data.Open, 'red', 'green');

title('AAPL Stock Price Candlestick Chart');

This code generates a candlestick chart to visualize the daily price movement of AAPL stock.

Technical Analysis

MATLAB ALLOWS YOU TO perform technical analysis on financial data. You can calculate common technical indicators like moving averages, relative strength index (RSI), and stochastic oscillators.

% Calculate 50-day moving average

ma_50 = movmean(data.Close, 50);

In this snippet, we compute the 50-day moving average of the closing prices of AAPL stock.

Portfolio Optimization

MATLAB'S FINANCIAL Toolbox includes tools for portfolio optimization, enabling you to build diversified portfolios that maximize returns while managing risk.

% Define asset returns and covariance matrix

returns = randn(100, 5); *% Simulated returns data*

covariance_matrix = cov(returns);

```
% Perform portfolio optimization

port = Portfolio;

port = setAssetMoments(port, mean(returns), covariance_matrix);

port = setDefaultConstraints(port);

weights = estimateFrontier(port, 20);
```

Here, we demonstrate a simplified example of portfolio optimization with random returns data.

Backtesting Trading Strategies

MATLAB IS ALSO WELL-suited for backtesting trading strategies. You can define trading rules, simulate trades, and evaluate the performance of your strategies.

```
% Define a simple moving average crossover strategy

short_ma = movmean(data.Close, 10);

long_ma = movmean(data.Close, 50);

buy_signal = short_ma > long_ma;

sell_signal = short_ma < long_ma;

% Simulate trades and calculate performance

positions = zeros(size(data, 1), 1);

positions(buy_signal) = 1;

positions(sell_signal) = -1;

returns = positions .* data.Close;
```

```
cumulative_returns = cumsum(returns);

% Evaluate strategy performance

sharpe_ratio = sharpe(returns, 0.03);
```

In this example, we create a basic moving average crossover trading strategy and assess its performance using metrics like the Sharpe ratio.

Risk Management

MANAGING RISK IS PARAMOUNT in financial analysis. MATLAB allows you to quantify and manage risk using various risk metrics and techniques.

```
% Calculate Value at Risk (VaR)

var_95 = quantile(returns, 0.05);
```

Here, we compute the 95% Value at Risk (VaR) for a portfolio.

In summary, MATLAB is a versatile platform for financial analysis, offering tools for data retrieval, visualization, technical analysis, portfolio optimization, backtesting trading strategies, and risk management. Whether you're a financial analyst, trader, or investor, MATLAB can enhance your decision-making processes in the complex world of finance.

Section 12.2: Risk Management Models

RISK MANAGEMENT IS a critical aspect of financial analysis and decision-making. MATLAB offers a range of tools and models to assess and mitigate risks associated with investments, portfolios, and financial instruments. In this section, we'll explore some of the risk management models and techniques available in MATLAB.

Value at Risk (VaR)

VALUE AT RISK (VAR) is a widely used risk metric that estimates the maximum potential loss an investment portfolio may incur over a specified time horizon with a certain level of confidence. MATLAB provides functions for calculating VaR using various methods, including historical simulation, parametric methods, and Monte Carlo simulation.

```
% Calculate VaR using historical simulation

returns = randn(100, 1); % Simulated returns data

confidence_level = 0.95; % 95% confidence level

var = quantile(returns, 1 - confidence_level);
```

In this example, we use historical simulation to estimate VaR for a portfolio with a 95% confidence level. The quantile function helps us determine the VaR.

Conditional Value at Risk (CVaR)

CONDITIONAL VALUE AT Risk (CVaR), also known as Expected Shortfall (ES), provides a more comprehensive measure of risk by considering the tail of the loss distribution beyond VaR. MATLAB allows you to compute CVaR easily.

```
% Calculate CVaR using historical data

cvar_level = 0.95; % 95% confidence level

sorted_returns = sort(returns, 'ascend');

cvar = mean(sorted_returns(1:round(cvar_level * length(returns))));
```

In this snippet, we compute CVaR at a 95% confidence level by averaging the returns in the tail of the distribution.

Portfolio Risk Metrics

WHEN MANAGING A PORTFOLIO, it's essential to assess its overall risk. MATLAB's Financial Toolbox provides functions to calculate various portfolio risk metrics, including standard deviation, beta, and tracking error.

```
% Calculate portfolio standard deviation and beta

port_returns = randn(100, 5); % Simulated portfolio returns data

port_weights = rand(5, 1); % Portfolio weights

port_std = std(port_returns * port_weights);

port_beta = beta(port_returns, port_weights, market_returns);
```

In this example, we calculate the portfolio standard deviation and beta using simulated data. The std and beta functions simplify these calculations.

Stress Testing

STRESS TESTING INVOLVES analyzing how a portfolio or financial instrument performs under extreme adverse conditions. MATLAB allows you to simulate and analyze stress scenarios to assess potential losses.

```
% Simulate stress scenarios

shock_factor = 0.2; % 20% market shock

stressed_returns = port_returns - shock_factor * market_returns;
```

```
% Calculate losses under stress scenarios

losses = sum(stressed_returns < 0);
```

Here, we simulate a market shock and calculate the losses incurred by the portfolio under stressed conditions.

Monte Carlo Simulation

MONTE CARLO SIMULATION is a powerful technique for risk assessment. MATLAB's capabilities in random number generation and simulation make it suitable for modeling complex financial instruments and portfolios.

```
% Monte Carlo simulation for option pricing

rng(123); % Set random seed for reproducibility

S0 = 100; % Initial stock price

K = 110; % Strike price

r = 0.05; % Risk-free rate

T = 1; % Time to maturity

volatility = 0.2; % Volatility

N = 1000; % Number of simulations

simulated_prices = zeros(N, 1);

for i = 1:N

stock_prices = simulate_stock_prices(S0, r, volatility, T);

option_payoff = max(stock_prices(end) - K, 0);

simulated_prices(i) = option_payoff * exp(-r * T);
```

```
end

% Calculate option price and risk metrics

option_price = mean(simulated_prices);

option_std = std(simulated_prices);
```

In this example, we use Monte Carlo simulation to price a European call option and calculate its risk metrics.

MATLAB's comprehensive risk management capabilities make it a valuable tool for financial professionals seeking to assess and mitigate risks in their investment portfolios and financial strategies. Whether you're managing a portfolio or analyzing individual financial instruments, MATLAB provides the tools you need to make informed risk-related decisions.

Section 12.3: Econometrics and Economic Modeling

ECONOMETRICS IS A FIELD of study that combines economics, statistics, and mathematics to analyze and model economic data. MATLAB provides powerful tools and functions for econometric analysis and economic modeling, making it a valuable resource for economists, researchers, and analysts. In this section, we'll explore some of the key econometric and economic modeling techniques available in MATLAB.

Time Series Analysis

TIME SERIES DATA, WHICH consists of observations collected over time, is prevalent in economics. MATLAB's Econometrics Toolbox offers a wide range of functions to analyze and model time series data. You can perform tasks such as:

- Importing and preprocessing time series data.
- Estimating and validating time series models, including autoregressive integrated moving average (ARIMA) models.
- Forecasting future values based on historical data.

```
% Example of time series analysis

data = xlsread('economic_data.xlsx'); % Load economic data from an Excel file

time_series = timeseries(data, 'Dates', datestr(datetime(2020,1,1):calmonths(1):datetime(2022,12,31), 'yyyy-mm')); % Create a time series object

mdl = arima(2,1,1); % Specify an ARIMA(2,1,1) model

estMdl = estimate(mdl, time_series); % Estimate the model parameters

forecasted_data = forecast(estMdl, 12); % Forecast the next 12 months
```

In this example, we load economic data from an Excel file, create a time series object, estimate an ARIMA(2,1,1) model, and then use it to forecast future data points.

Economic Modeling

MATLAB ALLOWS ECONOMISTS to build and analyze economic models, from simple linear models to complex systems of equations. You can use MATLAB for tasks like:

- Solving systems of equations to find equilibrium points.

- Simulating economic scenarios to analyze their impact.
- Estimating parameters for economic models.

```
% Example of solving a system of equations

syms x y;

eq1 = 2*x + 3*y == 10;

eq2 = x - 2*y == 5;

sol = solve([eq1, eq2], [x, y]);
```

In this snippet, we solve a system of linear equations to find the values of x and y that satisfy both equations.

Economic Data Visualization

VISUALIZING ECONOMIC data is crucial for understanding trends and patterns. MATLAB offers extensive plotting and visualization capabilities. You can create various types of plots, including time series plots, scatter plots, and heatmaps, to better understand economic data.

```
% Example of creating a time series plot

plot(time_series)

title('Economic Data Over Time')

xlabel('Date')

ylabel('Value')
```

This code generates a time series plot of economic data, making it easier to visualize trends and fluctuations over time.

Economic Forecasting

ECONOMIC FORECASTING involves predicting future economic conditions, such as GDP growth, inflation rates, or stock market performance. MATLAB's capabilities in time series analysis, regression analysis, and machine learning can be applied to build and validate forecasting models.

```
% Example of economic forecasting using a linear regression model

econ_data = readtable('economic_indicators.csv'); % Load economic data from a CSV file

model = fitlm(econ_data, 'GDP ~ UnemploymentRate + InflationRate + InterestRate'); % Build a linear regression model

forecasted_GDP = predict(model, new_data); % Predict future GDP based on new data
```

In this example, we load economic data from a CSV file, build a linear regression model to predict GDP, and then use the model to forecast GDP based on new economic indicators.

MATLAB's comprehensive toolbox for econometrics and economic modeling makes it an essential tool for economists and researchers working in the field of economics. Whether you need to analyze time series data, build economic models, visualize economic trends, or make economic forecasts, MATLAB provides the tools and flexibility to support your analysis and research.

Section 12.4: Operations Research and Optimization

OPERATIONS RESEARCH is a discipline that focuses on the application of mathematical modeling and optimization techniques to solve complex decision-making problems. MATLAB provides a robust set of optimization tools and libraries, making it a valuable platform for operations research practitioners and analysts. In this section, we'll explore how MATLAB can be used for various aspects of operations research, including linear and nonlinear optimization, integer programming, and network optimization.

Linear and Nonlinear Optimization

OPTIMIZATION PROBLEMS are pervasive in operations research, ranging from resource allocation to production planning. MATLAB's Optimization Toolbox offers a wide range of functions to tackle both linear and nonlinear optimization problems. You can formulate and solve optimization problems, subject to constraints and objectives.

```
% Example of solving a linear optimization problem

A = [3, 2; -1, 4]; % Coefficient matrix

b = [6; 3]; % Right-hand side vector

lb = [0; 0]; % Lower bounds on variables

[x, fval] = linprog([1; 2], -A, -b, [], [], lb); % Solve the linear optimization problem
```

In this example, we formulate and solve a simple linear optimization problem using the linprog function. MATLAB allows you to specify the objective function, inequality constraints, and variable bounds.

Integer Programming

INTEGER PROGRAMMING is used when decision variables are required to take integer values. MATLAB's Mixed-Integer Linear Programming (MILP) solver, available in the Optimization

Toolbox, can handle such problems. Integer programming is commonly used in problems like workforce scheduling and network design.

```
% Example of solving an integer programming problem

intcon = 1:3; % Specify which variables are integers

f = [-1; -2; -3]; % Coefficients of the objective function

Aeq = [1, 1, 2]; % Coefficient matrix for equality constraints

beq = 5; % Right-hand side of the equality constraint

lb = [0; 0; 0]; % Lower bounds on variables

[x, fval] = intlinprog(f, intcon, [], [], Aeq, beq, lb);
```

In this code snippet, we solve an integer programming problem using intlinprog. We specify which variables should be integers and provide the objective function, constraints, and bounds.

Network Optimization

NETWORK OPTIMIZATION problems involve finding the optimal flow of resources through a network, such as transportation or supply chain networks. MATLAB's Network Optimization Toolbox offers functions for solving network flow problems and other related tasks.

```
% Example of solving a transportation problem

cost = [5, 7, 6; 8, 6, 4; 3, 5, 9]; % Cost matrix

supply = [20; 30; 25]; % Supply at sources

demand = [15; 25; 35]; % Demand at destinations
```

```
[x, fval] = linprog(cost(:), [], [], kron(eye(3), ones(1, 3)), demand, zeros(9, 1), []);
```

Here, we demonstrate how to solve a transportation problem using linear programming. The cost matrix represents the transportation costs between sources and destinations, and we aim to minimize the total transportation cost while satisfying supply and demand constraints.

MATLAB's optimization capabilities extend to quadratic programming, mixed-integer nonlinear programming (MINLP), and more, making it a versatile tool for tackling various operations research problems. Whether you're optimizing logistics, resource allocation, or production planning, MATLAB provides the tools to find efficient solutions to complex decision-making problems in operations research.

Section 12.5: Business Intelligence and Data Analysis

BUSINESS INTELLIGENCE (BI) is a critical component of modern organizations, enabling data-driven decision-making and providing insights into business performance. MATLAB offers powerful tools for business intelligence, data analysis, and visualization, making it a valuable platform for extracting actionable insights from data. In this section, we'll explore how MATLAB can be used for various aspects of BI, including data exploration, statistical analysis, predictive analytics, and interactive reporting.

Data Exploration

DATA EXPLORATION IS the first step in the BI process, involving the discovery and understanding of data patterns and trends. MATLAB provides various functions and visualization tools to facilitate data exploration. You can load data from different sources, clean and preprocess it, and generate summary statistics and visualizations.

```
% Example of data exploration

data = readtable('sales_data.csv'); % Load data from a CSV file

summary(data); % Display summary statistics

histogram(data.Sales); % Create a histogram of sales data
```

In this example, we load data from a CSV file and use MATLAB's readtable function to create a data table. We then generate summary statistics and create a histogram to visualize the distribution of sales data.

Statistical Analysis

STATISTICAL ANALYSIS is a fundamental component of BI, helping organizations understand their data better. MATLAB provides a comprehensive set of statistical functions and tools for hypothesis testing, regression analysis, and multivariate analysis.

```
% Example of statistical analysis

x = randn(100, 1); % Generate random data

y = 2 * x + 0.5 * randn(100, 1); % Create a linear relationship with noise

mdl = fitlm(x, y); % Fit a linear regression model

disp(mdl); % Display regression model results
```

In this code snippet, we generate random data with a linear relationship and noise. We then use MATLAB's fitlm function to fit a linear regression model to the data and display the regression model results.

Predictive Analytics

PREDICTIVE ANALYTICS involves forecasting future trends and outcomes based on historical data. MATLAB's Machine Learning Toolbox provides a wide range of machine learning algorithms for predictive modeling, including decision trees, support vector machines, and neural networks.

```
% Example of predictive analytics

load fisheriris; % Load the Iris dataset

X = meas(:, 1:4); % Features

Y = species; % Target variable

mdl = fitcecoc(X, Y); % Fit a multiclass classifier

new_observation = [5.1, 3.5, 1.4, 0.2]; % New observation

predicted_species = predict(mdl, new_observation); % Predict the species

disp(predicted_species);
```

Here, we use MATLAB to perform predictive analytics on the Iris dataset. We load the data, fit a multiclass classifier using the fitcecoc function, and then predict the species of a new observation based on its features.

Interactive Reporting

EFFECTIVE BI OFTEN involves creating interactive reports and dashboards to communicate insights to stakeholders. MATLAB's capabilities for creating live scripts and interactive apps make it easy to generate dynamic reports and share them with others.

```
% Example of creating an interactive report

liveScript = matlab.desktop.editor.newLiveScript;

fprintf(liveScript, '# Sales Analysis Report\n\n');

fprintf(liveScript, '%% Summary Statistics\n');

fprintf(liveScript, 'data = readtable("sales_data.csv");\n');

fprintf(liveScript, 'summary(data);\n\n');

fprintf(liveScript, '%% Sales Trend Plot\n');

fprintf(liveScript, 'plot(data.Date, data.Sales);\n');

fprintf(liveScript, 'title("Sales Trend Over Time");\n');

liveScript.saveAs('SalesAnalysis.mlx');
```

In this example, we create an interactive report using a live script. We include code, text, and visualizations to provide a comprehensive analysis of sales data. Live scripts can be shared with others, allowing them to interact with the report and explore the data further.

MATLAB's versatility in data exploration, statistical analysis, predictive analytics, and interactive reporting makes it a valuable tool for business intelligence professionals and data analysts. Whether you're analyzing sales trends, forecasting demand, or creating interactive reports, MATLAB provides the tools to turn data into actionable insights that drive informed decision-making in organizations.

Chapter 13: Machine Learning and AI with MATLAB

Section 13.1: Introduction to Machine Learning in MATLAB

MACHINE LEARNING (ML) has revolutionized various industries by enabling computers to learn from data and make predictions or decisions without explicit programming. MATLAB offers a comprehensive ecosystem for machine learning and artificial intelligence (AI) that caters to beginners and experts alike. In this section, we'll introduce you to the world of machine learning in MATLAB, covering the fundamental concepts and tools at your disposal.

Understanding Machine Learning

AT ITS CORE, MACHINE learning is about creating algorithms that can generalize patterns from data to make predictions or decisions. It's divided into several subfields, including supervised learning, unsupervised learning, and reinforcement learning. MATLAB supports all these paradigms, making it versatile for a wide range of applications.

Getting Started with MATLAB for Machine Learning

TO GET STARTED WITH machine learning in MATLAB, you need to understand its basic components:

- **Data**: Machine learning starts with data. You'll need labeled data for supervised learning or unlabeled data for unsupervised learning. MATLAB allows you to import and preprocess data easily.

- **Feature Engineering**: Feature engineering involves selecting and transforming the relevant attributes (features) in your data. MATLAB provides tools for feature selection, extraction, and transformation.

- **Model Selection**: Choosing the right machine learning model is crucial. MATLAB offers an extensive set of pre-built models and algorithms for different tasks.

- **Training and Evaluation**: You'll train your model using a portion of your data and evaluate its performance on unseen data. MATLAB simplifies this process with functions for training, cross-validation, and testing.

Example of Supervised Learning in MATLAB

LET'S EXPLORE A SIMPLE example of supervised learning using MATLAB. We'll train a linear regression model to predict the price of houses based on their square footage.

```
% Load the dataset

data = readtable('house_prices.csv');

% Define features and target variable

X = data.SquareFootage;

y = data.Price;

% Split the data into training and testing sets

rng(1); % For reproducibility
```

```
cv = cvpartition(height(data), 'HoldOut', 0.2);

X_train = X(cv.training);

y_train = y(cv.training);

X_test = X(cv.test);

y_test = y(cv.test);

% Train a linear regression model

mdl = fitlm(X_train, y_train);

% Predict house prices on the test set

y_pred = predict(mdl, X_test);

% Evaluate the model

RMSE = sqrt(mean((y_test - y_pred).^2));

disp(['Root Mean Squared Error: ' num2str(RMSE)]);
```

In this code, we load a dataset, split it into training and testing sets, train a linear regression model, make predictions, and evaluate the model's performance using the root mean squared error (RMSE).

Machine learning in MATLAB is approachable, thanks to its rich documentation, built-in functions, and user-friendly interfaces. Whether you're new to ML or an experienced practitioner, MATLAB has the tools to help you build and deploy machine learning models for various real-world applications.

Section 13.2: Supervised Learning Techniques in MATLAB

SUPERVISED LEARNING is a subset of machine learning where the algorithm learns from labeled data. In this section, we will delve deeper into supervised learning techniques using MATLAB. MATLAB provides a plethora of tools and functions for supervised learning, making it an ideal environment to develop predictive models.

Classification and Regression

SUPERVISED LEARNING can be categorized into two main types: classification and regression.

- **Classification**: In classification tasks, the goal is to predict the class or category of a given input. For example, classifying emails as spam or not spam is a common classification problem. MATLAB supports a wide range of classification algorithms, such as decision trees, support vector machines, and neural networks.

- **Regression**: Regression aims to predict a continuous numerical value. For instance, predicting the price of a house based on its features falls under regression. MATLAB offers various regression techniques, including linear regression, support vector regression, and ensemble methods like random forests.

Example: Classification with MATLAB

LET'S ILLUSTRATE CLASSIFICATION using MATLAB with an example where we classify flowers into different species based on their petal and sepal measurements using the famous Iris dataset. We'll use a support vector machine (SVM) classifier for this task.

```
% Load the Iris dataset

load fisheriris;

% Define the predictors (features) and response (species)

X = meas;

Y = species;

% Split the data into training and testing sets

cv = cvpartition(Y,'HoldOut',0.3);

X_train = X(training(cv),:);

Y_train = Y(training(cv));

X_test = X(test(cv),:);

Y_test = Y(test(cv));

% Train a support vector machine classifier

mdl = fitcsvm(X_train, Y_train);

% Predict the species on the test set

Y_pred = predict(mdl, X_test);

% Evaluate the classifier

accuracy = sum(Y_pred == Y_test) / length(Y_test);

disp(['Classification Accuracy: ' num2str(accuracy)]);
```

In this code, we load the Iris dataset, split it into training and testing sets, train an SVM classifier, make predictions, and evaluate the classification accuracy.

Regression with MATLAB

FOR REGRESSION TASKS, MATLAB provides similar ease of use and versatility. Here's a simple example of linear regression using MATLAB to predict a student's final exam score based on the number of hours they studied:

```
% Load the dataset

data = readtable('exam_scores.csv');

% Define features and target variable

X = data.HoursStudied;

Y = data.ExamScore;

% Train a linear regression model

mdl = fitlm(X, Y);

% Predict the final exam score

hours_to_predict = [4, 6, 8];

predicted_scores = predict(mdl, hours_to_predict);

disp(['Predicted Scores: ' num2str(predicted_scores)]);
```

In this example, we load the dataset, train a linear regression model, and make predictions for different hours of study.

These examples highlight the simplicity and effectiveness of using MATLAB for both classification and regression tasks in supervised learning. With a wide range of algorithms and extensive documentation, MATLAB empowers users to tackle various real-world problems with confidence.

Section 13.3: Unsupervised Learning Approaches in MATLAB

UNSUPERVISED LEARNING is a branch of machine learning where the algorithm tries to find patterns or relationships within data without explicit supervision or labeled outcomes. This section explores various unsupervised learning techniques available in MATLAB, which are used for tasks like clustering and dimensionality reduction.

Clustering Techniques

CLUSTERING IS A COMMON unsupervised learning task that groups similar data points together. MATLAB offers several clustering algorithms:

- **K-Means Clustering**: This is one of the most widely used clustering algorithms. K-Means divides data points into 'K' clusters, minimizing the distance between data points within the same cluster.

```
% Example of K-Means clustering

X = randn(100,2); % Sample data

K = 3; % Number of clusters

[idx, C] = kmeans(X, K); % Cluster data into K clusters
```

- **Hierarchical Clustering**: Hierarchical clustering builds a tree-like structure of clusters, allowing you to visualize data at various levels of granularity.

```
% Example of Hierarchical Clustering

Z = linkage(X, 'ward'); % Create hierarchical clusters

dendrogram(Z); % Plot dendrogram
```

- **DBSCAN (Density-Based Spatial Clustering of Applications with Noise)**: DBSCAN identifies dense regions of data points separated by sparse regions, making it robust to outliers.

```
% Example of DBSCAN clustering

epsilon = 0.5; % Maximum distance between points in a cluster

minPts = 5; % Minimum number of points required to form a cluster

[idx, C] = dbscan(X, epsilon, minPts); % Cluster data using DBSCAN
```

Dimensionality Reduction

DIMENSIONALITY REDUCTION techniques are essential for simplifying and visualizing high-dimensional data. MATLAB provides tools for Principal Component Analysis (PCA) and t-Distributed Stochastic Neighbor Embedding (t-SNE):

- **Principal Component Analysis (PCA)**: PCA reduces the dimensionality of data while preserving as much variance as possible.

```
% Example of PCA
```

X = randn(100, 3); *% Sample data*

coeff = pca(X); *% Calculate PCA coefficients*

X_pca = X * coeff(:, 1:2); *% Reduce data to 2 principal components*

- **t-Distributed Stochastic Neighbor Embedding (t-SNE)**: t-SNE is used for visualizing high-dimensional data in a lower-dimensional space while preserving pairwise similarities.

% Example of t-SNE

Y = tsne(X); *% Perform t-SNE*

scatter(Y(:,1), Y(:,2)); *% Visualize the lower-dimensional representation*

Anomaly Detection

UNSUPERVISED LEARNING can also be applied to anomaly detection. MATLAB provides methods to identify data points that deviate significantly from the norm. For instance, the Gaussian Mixture Model (GMM) can be used for anomaly detection:

% Example of Anomaly Detection using GMM

X = [randn(100, 2); 10 + 2*randn(10, 2)]; *% Sample data with anomalies*

gmm = fitgmdist(X, 2); *% Fit a Gaussian Mixture Model*

idx = cluster(gmm, X); *% Cluster data points*

anomalies = X(idx == 2, :); *% Anomalies are points in the second cluster*

These examples showcase the versatility of unsupervised learning techniques available in MATLAB for tasks such as clustering, dimensionality reduction, and anomaly detection. MATLAB's user-friendly interface and extensive documentation make it a powerful platform for exploring and applying these methods to a wide range of real-world data analysis scenarios.

Section 13.4: Deep Learning and Neural Networks in MATLAB

DEEP LEARNING IS A subfield of machine learning that focuses on artificial neural networks, particularly deep neural networks with multiple layers. MATLAB provides comprehensive support for deep learning, making it a popular choice for researchers and practitioners in this field. In this section, we'll explore MATLAB's capabilities for deep learning.

Deep Learning Toolbox

MATLAB'S DEEP LEARNING Toolbox is a powerful environment for designing, training, and deploying neural networks. It offers a wide range of pre-trained models, optimization algorithms, and tools for visualizing and analyzing neural network architectures.

Building Neural Networks

YOU CAN CREATE CUSTOM neural networks using MATLAB's high-level neural network API. Here's a simple example of creating a feedforward neural network:

```
% Create a feedforward neural network

net = feedforwardnet(10); % 10 hidden neurons
```

Pre-trained Models

MATLAB PROVIDES ACCESS to a variety of pre-trained deep learning models, including popular architectures like AlexNet, VGG-16, and ResNet. These models can be fine-tuned for specific tasks or used for feature extraction.

```
% Load a pre-trained deep learning model

net = alexnet;
```

Transfer Learning

TRANSFER LEARNING IS a common technique in deep learning where you fine-tune a pre-trained model on a new dataset. MATLAB simplifies this process:

```
% Load a pre-trained model for transfer learning

net = resnet18;

% Load new data for fine-tuning

data = imageDatastore('new_data_directory');

% Fine-tune the model

options = trainingOptions('sgdm', 'MaxEpochs', 10);

new_net = trainNetwork(data, net, options);
```

Deep Learning Applications

DEEP LEARNING CAN BE applied to various tasks, including image classification, object detection, natural language processing, and more. MATLAB's toolbox supports a wide range of applications:

- **Image Classification**: You can train deep neural networks to classify images into multiple categories using tools like trainNetwork and classify.

```
% Example of image classification

data = imageDatastore('image_data_directory');

net = alexnet;

options = trainingOptions('sgdm', 'MaxEpochs', 10);

trained_net = trainNetwork(data, net, options);
```

- **Object Detection**: MATLAB supports object detection tasks with pre-trained models like YOLO and Faster R-CNN.

```
% Example of object detection

data = imageDatastore('object_data_directory');

detector = trainYOLOv2ObjectDetector(data, 'Darknet53');
```

- **Natural Language Processing**: You can build and train recurrent neural networks (RNNs) and transformers for text analysis and language generation.

```
% Example of text generation using LSTM

textData = preprocessTextData('text_data.txt');

net = lstmNetwork(128, 'SequenceLength', 20);
```

```
options = trainingOptions('adam', 'MaxEpochs', 50);

trained_net = trainNetwork(textData, net, options);
```

Deep Learning Visualization and Analysis

MATLAB PROVIDES TOOLS for visualizing and analyzing deep learning models, including layer visualization, training progress plots, and techniques for debugging and improving network performance.

```
% Visualize layers of a neural network

analyzeNetwork(net);

% Plot training progress

plotTrainingProgress(info);
```

MATLAB's deep learning capabilities, combined with its user-friendly interface, make it a versatile platform for research and practical applications in the field of deep learning. Researchers and engineers can leverage these tools to develop and deploy neural networks for a wide range of tasks.

Section 13.5: Natural Language Processing with MATLAB

NATURAL LANGUAGE PROCESSING (NLP) is a subfield of artificial intelligence that focuses on the interaction between computers and human language. It encompasses a wide range of tasks, from text analysis and sentiment analysis to machine translation and chatbot development. MATLAB provides powerful tools and libraries for NLP, making it a valuable resource for researchers and developers in this field.

Text Processing

MATLAB ALLOWS YOU TO perform various text processing tasks, such as text cleaning, tokenization, and stemming, with ease.

Text Cleaning

```
% CLEAN AND PREPROCESS text data

text = "This is an example sentence with punctuation!";

cleanedText = lower(text); % Convert to lowercase

cleanedText = regexprep(cleanedText, '[^\w\s]', ''); % Remove punctuation
```

Tokenization

```
% TOKENIZE A TEXT INTO words

tokenizer = tokenizedDocument(cleanedText);

tokens = tokens(tokenizer);
```

Stemming

```
% APPLY STEMMING TO reduce words to their root form

stemmer = porterStemmer;

stemmedWords = erasePunctuation(tokens);

stemmedWords = normalizeWords(stemmer, stemmedWords);
```

Sentiment Analysis

SENTIMENT ANALYSIS is the process of determining the emotional tone or sentiment expressed in text data. MATLAB provides pre-trained models and functions for sentiment analysis.

```
% Perform sentiment analysis on text

sentimentModel = pretrainedTextSentimentModel("sentiment140");

sentimentScores = analyzeSentiment(sentimentModel, cleanedText);
```

Text Classification

TEXT CLASSIFICATION involves assigning predefined categories or labels to text documents. MATLAB's Text Analytics Toolbox simplifies this task.

```
% Train a text classifier

documents = tokenizedDocument(trainingTexts);

labels = categorical(trainingLabels);

classifier = trainTextClassifier(documents, labels);
```

Language Translation

MACHINE TRANSLATION is another important NLP task. MATLAB offers translation capabilities using pre-trained models.

```
% Translate text from one language to another

translator = machineTranslator("English", "French");

translatedText = translate(translator, "Hello, world!");
```

Chatbot Development

DEVELOPING CHATBOTS for customer support or virtual assistants is made easier with MATLAB. You can use NLP models and tools to create conversational agents.

```
% Create a simple chatbot

responses = ["Hello!", "How can I assist you today?", "Goodbye!"];

chatbot = chatBot(responses);
```

Text Generation

TEXT GENERATION MODELS, such as LSTM networks, can be used to generate human-like text. This can be applied to chatbots, creative writing, and more.

```
% Generate text using an LSTM network

textData = preprocessTextData('text_corpus.txt');

net = lstmNetwork(128, 'SequenceLength', 20);

options = trainingOptions('adam', 'MaxEpochs', 50);

trainedNet = trainNetwork(textData, net, options);

generatedText = generateText(trainedNet, 'SeedText', 'Once upon a time');
```

MATLAB's comprehensive support for NLP tasks, combined with its integration with other machine learning and deep learning capabilities, makes it a valuable tool for researchers and developers working on language-related applications. Whether it's analyzing text sentiment, developing chatbots, or translating languages,

MATLAB offers a wide range of functions and pre-trained models to streamline the NLP workflow.

Section 14.1: Digital Signal Processing Fundamentals

DIGITAL SIGNAL PROCESSING (DSP) is a fundamental concept in various engineering and scientific fields, including audio and image processing, telecommunications, and control systems. In this section, we'll explore the basics of DSP and how MATLAB can be used to perform essential DSP tasks.

Understanding Signals

IN DSP, SIGNALS ARE representations of data that vary with time, space, or some other independent variable. They can be categorized as continuous-time signals (analog signals) or discrete-time signals. MATLAB primarily deals with discrete-time signals, which are sequences of values sampled at specific time intervals.

Signal Representation in MATLAB

IN MATLAB, DISCRETE-time signals are typically represented as vectors or arrays. Each element of the vector corresponds to a value of the signal at a specific time or sample index. Here's an example of a simple discrete-time signal:

```
% Creating a simple discrete-time signal

t = 0:0.1:10; % Time vector from 0 to 10 with a step of 0.1

x = sin(t); % A sine wave signal
```

Signal Visualization

VISUALIZING SIGNALS is crucial for understanding their characteristics. MATLAB provides various plotting functions to visualize signals.

```
% Plotting a discrete-time signal

plot(t, x);

title('Sine Wave Signal');

xlabel('Time (s)');

ylabel('Amplitude');

grid on;
```

Signal Operations

DSP OFTEN INVOLVES operations such as filtering, convolution, and spectral analysis. MATLAB offers built-in functions and tools to perform these operations efficiently.

Filtering

```
% DESIGNING AND APPLYING a digital filter

Fs = 1000; % Sampling frequency (Hz)

Fpass = 100; % Passband frequency (Hz)

Fstop = 200; % Stopband frequency (Hz)

Ap = 0.5; % Passband ripple (dB)

Ast = 60; % Stopband attenuation (dB)
```

```
filterSpecs = fdesign.lowpass('Fp,Fst,Ap,Ast', Fpass, Fstop, Ap, Ast, Fs);

digitalFilter = design(filterSpecs, 'equiripple');

filteredSignal = filter(digitalFilter, x);
```

Convolution

```
% PERFORMING CONVOLUTION

h = [1, 2, 1]; % Impulse response of the system

y = conv(x, h); % Convolution of x and h
```

Spectral Analysis

SPECTRAL ANALYSIS HELPS in understanding the frequency components of a signal. MATLAB provides functions like fft and periodogram for spectral analysis.

```
% Computing and plotting the power spectral density

[Pxx, f] = periodogram(x, [], [], Fs);

plot(f, 10*log10(Pxx));

title('Power Spectral Density');

xlabel('Frequency (Hz)');

ylabel('Power/Frequency (dB/Hz)');
```

Digital Signal Processing is a broad field with applications in various domains. MATLAB's comprehensive toolbox for DSP, along with its capabilities for signal visualization, filtering, convolution, and spectral analysis, makes it a powerful tool for engineers and researchers working on signal processing tasks. In the upcoming sections, we will delve deeper into specific DSP applications and techniques using MATLAB.

Section 14.2: Image Enhancement and Filtering

IMAGE ENHANCEMENT IS a critical aspect of digital image processing, aimed at improving the quality of an image for better visualization or analysis. In this section, we will explore image enhancement techniques using MATLAB, including filtering methods.

Image Enhancement Techniques

Histogram Equalization

HISTOGRAM EQUALIZATION is a simple yet effective method to enhance the contrast of an image. It redistributes the pixel intensity values in an image, making it more balanced across the entire dynamic range. MATLAB provides a built-in function for histogram equalization.

```
% Histogram equalization

originalImage = imread('input_image.jpg');

enhancedImage = histeq(originalImage);
```

Contrast Stretching

CONTRAST STRETCHING is another technique to enhance image contrast. It linearly scales the pixel intensity values to cover the full dynamic range.

```
% Contrast stretching

lowClip = 50; % Lower clipping percentage

highClip = 95; % Upper clipping percentage

enhancedImage = imadjust(originalImage, [lowClip/100, highClip/100], []);
```

Image Filtering

FILTERING IS A FUNDAMENTAL operation in image processing that involves applying a filter (kernel) to an image. MATLAB provides various filtering functions for tasks such as noise reduction and feature enhancement.

Gaussian Filtering

GAUSSIAN FILTERING is commonly used for noise reduction and blurring. It smooths an image by convolving it with a Gaussian kernel.

```
% Gaussian filtering

sigma = 1.5; % Standard deviation of the Gaussian kernel

filteredImage = imgaussfilt(originalImage, sigma);
```

Sharpening

IMAGE SHARPENING ENHANCES the fine details and edges in an image. MATLAB offers sharpening filters like the Laplacian filter.

```
% Sharpening using Laplacian filter

sharpened = imsharpen(originalImage);
```

Displaying Enhanced Images

AFTER APPLYING IMAGE enhancement techniques, it's essential to visualize the results.

```
% Displaying original and enhanced images

subplot(1, 2, 1);

imshow(originalImage);

title('Original Image');

subplot(1, 2, 2);

imshow(enhancedImage);

title('Enhanced Image');
```

Image enhancement and filtering are crucial in various applications, including medical imaging, computer vision, and satellite image analysis. MATLAB's extensive image processing toolbox simplifies the implementation of these techniques, allowing researchers and engineers to achieve improved image quality and better insights from their data. In the next section, we will delve further into advanced image processing techniques using MATLAB.

Section 14.3: Feature Extraction Techniques

FEATURE EXTRACTION plays a crucial role in image processing and computer vision applications. It involves identifying and extracting relevant information or features from an image to facilitate further analysis and decision-making. In this section, we will explore various feature extraction techniques using MATLAB.

Edge Detection

EDGE DETECTION IS A fundamental step in feature extraction, as it helps identify object boundaries and key features within an image. MATLAB offers several edge detection methods, with the Canny edge detector being one of the most commonly used.

```
% Edge detection using the Canny method

originalImage = imread('input_image.jpg');

edges = edge(rgb2gray(originalImage), 'Canny');
```

Blob Detection

BLOB DETECTION IS USED to identify regions or objects with specific characteristics, such as size or intensity. MATLAB provides functions like regionprops to extract properties of detected blobs, such as centroid coordinates, area, and bounding boxes.

```
% Blob detection and feature extraction

bwImage = im2bw(originalImage, graythresh(originalImage));

labeledImage = bwlabel(bwImage);

blobMeasurements = regionprops(labeledImage, 'all');
```

Corner Detection

CORNER DETECTION IS essential for recognizing unique points in an image. MATLAB includes corner detection algorithms like the Harris corner detector, which can identify corners based on local intensity variations.

```
% Corner detection using the Harris method

corners = detectHarrisFeatures(rgb2gray(originalImage));
```

Texture Analysis

TEXTURE ANALYSIS INVOLVES characterizing the spatial arrangement of pixel intensities in an image region. MATLAB offers tools like the Gray-Level Co-occurrence Matrix (GLCM) to extract texture features.

```
% Texture analysis using GLCM

grayImage = rgb2gray(originalImage);

glcm = graycomatrix(grayImage, 'Offset', [0 1; -1 1; -1 0; -1 -1]);

stats = graycoprops(glcm, {'Contrast', 'Correlation', 'Energy', 'Homogeneity'});
```

Color Histograms

COLOR HISTOGRAMS REPRESENT the distribution of color values in an image. They are useful for tasks such as object recognition and image retrieval. MATLAB allows you to compute and analyze color histograms easily.

```
% Color histogram computation

histR = imhist(originalImage(:,:,1));
```

```
histG = imhist(originalImage(:,:,2));

histB = imhist(originalImage(:,:,3));
```

Fourier Transform for Frequency Features

THE FOURIER TRANSFORM can extract frequency-domain features from an image. It is particularly useful for tasks like image denoising or analyzing periodic patterns.

```
% Fourier Transform for frequency analysis

fftImage = fft2(rgb2gray(originalImage));

fftShifted = fftshift(fftImage);
```

Feature extraction is a crucial step in image analysis, computer vision, and machine learning applications. MATLAB's extensive toolbox simplifies the process of extracting relevant information from images, enabling researchers and engineers to build robust systems for object detection, classification, and more. In the following section, we will explore computer vision techniques and applications using MATLAB.

Section 14.4: Computer Vision with MATLAB

COMPUTER VISION IS a field of study that focuses on enabling machines to interpret and understand visual information from the world around them. MATLAB provides a powerful platform for developing computer vision applications, offering a wide range of tools and libraries for image and video processing, object detection, and tracking. In this section, we will delve into the capabilities of MATLAB for computer vision.

Image Processing Toolbox

MATLAB'S IMAGE PROCESSING Toolbox is a fundamental resource for computer vision tasks. It provides functions for image enhancement, filtering, and manipulation. Here's an example of applying image enhancement:

```
% Image enhancement using histogram equalization

originalImage = imread('input_image.jpg');

enhancedImage = histeq(rgb2gray(originalImage));
```

Object Detection and Recognition

OBJECT DETECTION AND recognition are essential in computer vision applications. MATLAB offers pre-trained deep learning models, such as YOLO (You Only Look Once) and Faster R-CNN (Region-based Convolutional Neural Network), which can be used for object detection.

```
% Object detection using a pre-trained YOLO model

net = yolov3;

inputImage = imread('input_image.jpg');

detections = detect(net, inputImage);
```

Optical Character Recognition (OCR)

MATLAB'S OCR CAPABILITIES make it easy to extract text from images and recognize characters. This is particularly useful for tasks like reading text from images of documents or license plates.

```
% Optical Character Recognition (OCR)
```

```
ocrResults = ocr(originalImage);

recognizedText = ocrResults.Text;
```

Motion Detection and Tracking

MATLAB ALLOWS YOU TO perform motion detection and object tracking in videos or sequences of images. You can use background subtraction and Kalman filters for tracking objects.

```
% Motion detection and object tracking

videoReader = VideoReader('input_video.mp4');

foregroundDetector = vision.ForegroundDetector();

kalmanFilter = vision.KalmanFilter();
```

3D Vision and Stereo Vision

FOR APPLICATIONS INVOLVING depth perception, MATLAB supports 3D vision and stereo vision techniques. You can calibrate cameras and reconstruct 3D scenes from stereo image pairs.

```
% 3D vision and stereo vision

stereoParams = stereoParameters();

stereoImagePair = imread('stereo_image_pair.jpg');

pointCloud = reconstructScene(stereoImagePair, stereoParams);
```

Augmented Reality (AR)

AUGMENTED REALITY COMBINES the real world with computer-generated elements. MATLAB allows you to create AR applications by overlaying virtual objects on live camera feeds.

```
% Augmented Reality (AR) with MATLAB

augmentedRealityObject = augmentedRealityObject('model.obj');

augmentedRealityViewer = augmentedRealityViewer('Camera', 'AxesVisible', true);

show(augmentedRealityViewer, augmentedRealityObject);
```

MATLAB's rich set of functions, toolboxes, and pre-trained models make it a valuable platform for developing computer vision solutions. Whether you are working on image processing, object detection, or augmented reality, MATLAB provides the necessary tools and resources to streamline your development process. In the next section, we will explore audio processing and analysis with MATLAB.

Section 14.5: Audio Processing and Analysis with MATLAB

AUDIO PROCESSING AND analysis play a crucial role in various applications, from speech recognition and music processing to noise reduction and audio effects. MATLAB provides a comprehensive set of tools and functions for working with audio data, making it a versatile platform for audio-related tasks.

Importing and Reading Audio Files

MATLAB ALLOWS YOU TO import and read audio files in various formats, including WAV, MP3, and FLAC. You can use the audioread function to load audio data from a file.

```
% Importing and reading an audio file

[audioData, sampleRate] = audioread('audio_file.wav');
```

Basic Audio Manipulations

YOU CAN PERFORM BASIC operations on audio data, such as resampling, trimming, and mixing. Here's an example of resampling audio to a different sample rate:

```
% Resampling audio data

newSampleRate = 44100; % New sample rate in Hz

resampledAudio = resample(audioData, newSampleRate, sampleRate);
```

Audio Spectrogram and Visualization

VISUALIZING AUDIO DATA is essential for analysis. MATLAB's spectrogram function can generate a spectrogram, which provides insights into the frequency content of the audio signal.

```
% Creating a spectrogram

windowLength = 1024;

overlap = 512;

spectrogram(audioData, windowLength, overlap, [], sampleRate, 'yaxis');
```

Speech Recognition

MATLAB INCLUDES SPEECH recognition capabilities using the Speech Recognition Toolbox. You can recognize speech from audio signals and convert it into text.

```
% Speech recognition
```

speechRecognizer = speechClient('GoogleSpeechRecognition');

recognizedText = recognize(speechRecognizer, audioData, sampleRate);

Audio Effects and Filters

YOU CAN APPLY VARIOUS audio effects and filters to modify audio signals. MATLAB offers tools for equalization, noise reduction, and audio enhancement.

% Applying audio effects

equalizedAudio = equalizer(audioData, 'bass', 'Boost', 'mid', 'Cut');

denoisedAudio = denoiseAudio(audioData, 'Method', 'Wiener');

Music Analysis and Beat Detection

FOR MUSIC-RELATED TASKS, MATLAB provides functions to analyze musical attributes like tempo, beats, and pitch. Beat detection is particularly useful for rhythm analysis.

% Beat detection in music

tempo = estimateTempo(audioData, sampleRate);

beatLocations = beatTrack(audioData, sampleRate, 'Tempo', tempo);

Real-Time Audio Processing

MATLAB SUPPORTS REAL-time audio processing by interfacing with audio input and output devices. You can create audio streams for real-time applications like audio synthesis or live effects processing.

```
% Real-time audio processing

inputStream = audioDeviceReader('SampleRate', sampleRate);

outputStream = audioDeviceWriter('SampleRate', sampleRate);

while true

audioFrame = inputStream();

processedAudio = processAudio(audioFrame); % Your custom processing function

outputStream(processedAudio);

end
```

MATLAB's extensive capabilities in audio processing and analysis make it a valuable tool for a wide range of applications, from music production and speech recognition to acoustic measurements and sound engineering. Whether you're a musician, audio engineer, or researcher, MATLAB provides the tools needed to work with audio data effectively.

Chapter 15: Biomedical Applications of MATLAB

Biomedical applications of MATLAB encompass a wide range of domains, from signal processing in medical devices to modeling complex biological systems. MATLAB's versatility and powerful toolboxes make it a valuable resource for researchers and professionals in the biomedical field. In this chapter, we'll explore some of the key applications of MATLAB in biomedical engineering and research.

Section 15.1: Biomedical Signal Processing

BIOMEDICAL SIGNAL PROCESSING involves the analysis and manipulation of physiological signals such as electrocardiograms (ECG), electromyograms (EMG), and electroencephalograms (EEG). MATLAB provides various tools and techniques for processing and analyzing these signals.

Importing and Visualizing Biomedical Signals

YOU CAN USE MATLAB to import and visualize biomedical signals stored in various file formats. The plot function, combined with appropriate signal processing toolboxes, allows you to create informative plots and visualizations.

```
% Importing and plotting an ECG signal

ecgData = load('ecg_signal.mat');

time = 1:length(ecgData);

plot(time, ecgData);
```

```
xlabel('Time (s)');

ylabel('Amplitude (mV)');

title('ECG Signal');
```

Filtering and Denoising

BIOMEDICAL SIGNALS are often contaminated with noise. MATLAB provides a range of filtering techniques to remove noise and enhance the quality of the signals. For instance, you can design and apply digital filters to an ECG signal.

```
% Filtering an ECG signal

filteredECG = filterECG(ecgData, 'Bandpass', [0.5 50]);
```

Feature Extraction

FEATURE EXTRACTION is crucial for extracting meaningful information from biomedical signals. MATLAB offers functions for extracting features like R-peaks from ECG signals or spectral features from EEG signals.

```
% Extracting R-peaks from an ECG signal

rpeaks = detectRPeaks(ecgData, 'SampleRate', 1000);
```

Heart Rate Variability Analysis

HEART RATE VARIABILITY (HRV) analysis is a common technique in cardiology. MATLAB provides tools for HRV analysis, allowing you to assess the autonomic nervous system's activity.

```
% Calculate HRV parameters
```

```
hrvParams = computeHRVParameters(ecgData, 'SampleRate', 1000);
```

EEG Signal Processing

ELECTROENCEPHALOGRAMS (EEG) record brain activity. MATLAB can be used for preprocessing EEG data, event-related potential (ERP) analysis, and brain connectivity analysis.

```
% EEG preprocessing and analysis

eegData = load('eeg_data.mat');

cleanedEEG = preprocessEEG(eegData);

erpAnalysisResults = erpAnalysis(cleanedEEG);

connectivityMatrix = calculateConnectivity(cleanedEEG);
```

Integration with Machine Learning

BIOMEDICAL SIGNAL DATA can be integrated with machine learning techniques for tasks like disease classification or anomaly detection. MATLAB's machine learning toolbox simplifies this process.

```
% Machine learning for disease classification

X = extractFeatures(ecgData); % Extract features

y = labelData(ecgData); % Label data

model = trainClassifier(X, y); % Train a classifier
```

Biomedical signal processing in MATLAB opens up avenues for various research and clinical applications. Researchers and healthcare professionals can leverage MATLAB's capabilities to analyze data, develop diagnostic tools, and gain insights into complex physiological phenomena. From cardiology to neurology, MATLAB serves as a versatile platform for advancing biomedical research and improving healthcare outcomes.

Section 15.2: Medical Image Analysis

MEDICAL IMAGE ANALYSIS plays a pivotal role in diagnosing diseases, planning surgeries, and monitoring treatment progress. MATLAB offers an extensive set of tools and algorithms for processing and analyzing various types of medical images, including X-rays, MRIs, CT scans, and histological images.

Image Preprocessing

BEFORE ANY ANALYSIS, medical images often require preprocessing to enhance their quality and remove artifacts. MATLAB provides functions for tasks such as noise reduction, contrast enhancement, and image registration.

```
% Image denoising and enhancement

noisyImage = imread('noisy_xray.png');

denoisedImage = denoiseImage(noisyImage);

enhancedImage = enhanceContrast(denoisedImage);
```

Segmentation

SEGMENTATION IS THE process of partitioning an image into meaningful regions or objects. MATLAB's segmentation algorithms can be applied to identify and isolate structures of interest, such as tumors in MRI scans or blood vessels in angiograms.

```
% Tumor segmentation in an MRI scan

mriImage = imread('brain_mri.png');

tumorMask = segmentTumor(mriImage);
```

Feature Extraction

FEATURE EXTRACTION from medical images is essential for quantifying characteristics relevant to diagnosis. MATLAB offers functions to extract features like texture, shape, and intensity statistics from image regions.

```
% Texture feature extraction

roi = selectRegionOfInterest(mriImage);

textureFeatures = extractTextureFeatures(roi);
```

Image Registration

IN MEDICAL IMAGING, it's common to align images from different modalities or time points. MATLAB provides tools for image registration, ensuring accurate spatial alignment.

```
% Registering pre- and post-treatment images

preTreatmentImage = imread('pre_treatment_ct.png');

postTreatmentImage = imread('post_treatment_ct.png');

registeredImage = registerImages(preTreatmentImage, postTreatmentImage);
```

3D Image Analysis

MANY MEDICAL IMAGES are 3D volumes, such as CT or MRI scans. MATLAB's capabilities extend to 3D image analysis, enabling volumetric rendering, segmentation, and measurement.

```
% 3D visualization and analysis of a CT scan

ctVolume = loadCTVolume('patient_ct.nii');

renderedVolume = render3DVolume(ctVolume);

tumorVolume = segmentTumor3D(ctVolume);

tumorVolumeStats = measureTumorVolume(tumorVolume);
```

Deep Learning for Medical Image Analysis

DEEP LEARNING HAS REVOLUTIONIZED medical image analysis, and MATLAB provides tools for training and deploying deep neural networks. Convolutional neural networks (CNNs) can be employed for tasks like disease detection, image synthesis, and organ segmentation.

```
% Deep learning for lung nodule detection

lungCTImages = loadCTDataset('lung_ct_images/');

labels = loadLabels('lung_nodule_labels.csv');

lungNoduleDetector = trainCNN(lungCTImages, labels);
```

Medical image analysis in MATLAB is not limited to these examples but extends to various domains, including radiology, pathology, and neuroscience. Researchers and medical professionals can harness MATLAB's capabilities to automate image analysis, extract quantitative information, and develop innovative diagnostic and treatment solutions. Whether for early disease detection or treatment planning, MATLAB serves as a powerful platform for advancing medical imaging and improving patient care.

Section 15.3: Modeling Biological Systems

MATHEMATICAL MODELING of biological systems is a crucial aspect of biomedical research and healthcare. MATLAB provides a versatile environment for creating, simulating, and analyzing models of biological processes, ranging from simple biochemical reactions to complex physiological systems.

Biochemical Reaction Modeling

ONE COMMON APPLICATION of MATLAB in biology is simulating biochemical reactions. You can use MATLAB to model the interactions between different chemical species, reactions rates, and concentration changes over time. This is particularly valuable in studying enzyme kinetics, metabolic pathways, and gene regulation.

```
% Example of a simple enzymatic reaction model

function dydt = enzymaticReaction(t, y)

% Parameters

k1 = 0.1;

k2 = 0.2;

% Initial concentrations

A = y(1);

B = y(2);
```

```
% Differential equations

dA = -k1 * A;

dB = k1 * A - k2 * B;

dydt = [dA; dB];

end

% Simulation

tspan = [0 10];

y0 = [1; 0];

[t, y] = ode45(@enzymaticReaction, tspan, y0);

% Plotting results

plot(t, y(:, 1), 'r', t, y(:, 2), 'b');

xlabel('Time');

ylabel('Concentration');

legend('A', 'B');

title('Enzymatic Reaction Simulation');
```

Biological Network Modeling

IN SYSTEMS BIOLOGY, researchers often deal with complex networks of interactions. MATLAB allows you to construct mathematical models of biological networks, such as gene regulatory networks or protein-protein interaction networks. You can then simulate these models to gain insights into their behavior.

```
% Example of a simple gene regulatory network model
```

```
function dydt = geneRegulation(t, y)
% Parameters
alpha = 0.1;
beta = 0.2;
gamma = 0.3;
delta = 0.4;
% Initial concentrations
mRNA = y(1);
protein = y(2);
% Differential equations
dmRNA = alpha - beta * mRNA;
dProtein = gamma * mRNA - delta * protein;
dydt = [dmRNA; dProtein];
end
% Simulation
tspan = [0 100];
y0 = [0; 0];
[t, y] = ode45(@geneRegulation, tspan, y0);
% Plotting results
plot(t, y(:, 1), 'r', t, y(:, 2), 'b');
```

```
xlabel('Time');
ylabel('Concentration');
legend('mRNA', 'Protein');
title('Gene Regulatory Network Simulation');
```

Pharmacokinetic Modeling

PHARMACOKINETICS INVOLVES studying the absorption, distribution, metabolism, and excretion (ADME) of drugs within the body. MATLAB is widely used for modeling drug pharmacokinetics, optimizing dosing regimens, and predicting drug concentrations in different tissues over time.

```
% Example of a two-compartment pharmacokinetic model
function dydt = pharmacokinetics(t, y)
% Parameters
ka = 0.2; % Absorption rate constant
k12 = 0.5; % Rate constant from compartment 1 to compartment 2
k21 = 0.3; % Rate constant from compartment 2 to compartment 1
% Initial concentrations
C1 = y(1);
C2 = y(2);
% Differential equations
dC1 = -ka * C1 + k21 * C2;
dC2 = k12 * C1 - k21 * C2;
```

```
dydt = [dC1; dC2];

end

% Simulation

tspan = [0 10];

y0 = [100; 0];

[t, y] = ode45(@pharmacokinetics, tspan, y0);

% Plotting results

plot(t, y(:, 1), 'r', t, y(:, 2), 'b');

xlabel('Time');

ylabel('Concentration');

legend('Compartment 1', 'Compartment 2');

title('Pharmacokinetic Model Simulation');
```

MATLAB's capabilities in modeling biological systems are not limited to these examples. Researchers and biologists can leverage MATLAB's extensive toolboxes and libraries for systems biology, computational biology, and pharmacokinetics to advance their understanding of complex biological phenomena and drive innovations in healthcare and biotechnology.

Section 15.4: Bioinformatics with MATLAB

BIOINFORMATICS IS A multidisciplinary field that combines biology, computer science, and mathematics to analyze and interpret biological data. MATLAB is a powerful tool for performing a wide range of bioinformatics tasks, from sequence analysis to structural biology and genomics.

Sequence Analysis

ONE OF THE FUNDAMENTAL tasks in bioinformatics is the analysis of biological sequences, such as DNA, RNA, and protein sequences. MATLAB provides various functions and toolboxes for sequence alignment, motif searching, and secondary structure prediction.

```
% Example of DNA sequence alignment

seq1 = 'ACGTAGTACGTAGTACGTAGT';

seq2 = 'AGTACGTAGTACGTCGATCG';

alignment = nwalign(seq1, seq2);

disp(['Sequence Alignment Score: ', num2str(alignment)]);
```

Structural Biology

IN STRUCTURAL BIOLOGY, researchers aim to understand the three-dimensional structures of biomolecules, such as proteins and nucleic acids. MATLAB can be used for tasks like molecular dynamics simulations, structure visualization, and docking studies.

```
% Example of protein structure visualization

pdbStruct = pdbread('1ake.pdb');

protein = trimerize(pdbStruct.Model.Atom, 3); % Trimerize the protein

figure;
```

```
show(protein);

title('Protein Structure Visualization');
```

Genomics and Transcriptomics

MATLAB PROVIDES TOOLS for analyzing large-scale genomics and transcriptomics data. You can perform tasks like differential gene expression analysis, functional enrichment analysis, and pathway analysis using appropriate toolboxes and libraries.

```
% Example of differential gene expression analysis

geneExpressionData = importdata('gene_expression_data.csv');

conditions = {'Control', 'Treatment'};

groups = [1, 2];

[~, pValues] = ttest2(geneExpressionData(:, groups(1)), geneExpressionData(:, groups(2)));

significantGenes = find(pValues < 0.05);

disp(['Significant genes: ', num2str(significantGenes)]);
```

Metabolomics and Systems Biology

METABOLOMICS IS THE study of small molecules (metabolites) in biological systems. MATLAB can be used for metabolomics data preprocessing, statistical analysis, and metabolic pathway modeling.

```
% Example of metabolic pathway modeling

pathwayModel = sbiomodel('MetabolicPathway');

reaction1 = addreaction(pathwayModel, 'A + B -> C');
```

```
reaction2 = addreaction(pathwayModel, 'C -> D + E');

kineticLaw1 = addkineticlaw(reaction1, 'MassAction');

kineticLaw2 = addkineticlaw(reaction2, 'MassAction');

parameter1 = addparameter(kineticLaw1, 'k1', 0.1);

parameter2 = addparameter(kineticLaw2, 'k2', 0.2);
```

Next-Generation Sequencing (NGS) Data Analysis

WITH THE ADVENT OF NGS technologies, analyzing DNA and RNA sequencing data has become crucial in genomics research. MATLAB offers toolboxes for handling NGS data, including read mapping, variant calling, and ChIP-seq analysis.

```
% Example of read mapping using the Bioinformatics Toolbox

genome = 'hg38'; % Human reference genome

reads = fastqread('sample_reads.fastq');

index = bowtie2index(genome);

alignedReads = bowtie2(index, reads);
```

In summary, MATLAB is a versatile platform for various bioinformatics tasks, making it an essential tool for researchers and scientists working in the fields of biology, genomics, and structural biology. Its capabilities in data analysis, visualization, and modeling empower scientists to extract valuable insights from complex biological data, ultimately contributing to advancements in our understanding of life sciences.

Section 15.5: Biomechanics and Movement

Analysis

BIOMECHANICS IS A FIELD of study that focuses on the mechanical aspects of living organisms, including the analysis of their movements and the forces acting on them. MATLAB is a powerful tool for conducting biomechanical research, enabling researchers to analyze and model various aspects of human and animal movement.

Motion Capture and Analysis

MOTION CAPTURE IS A common technique used to record and analyze human and animal movements. MATLAB can process motion capture data to extract valuable insights such as joint angles, gait analysis, and muscle forces.

```
% Example of motion capture data analysis

motionData = load('motion_capture_data.mat');

jointAngles = calculateJointAngles(motionData);

gaitAnalysisResults = analyzeGait(jointAngles);

muscleForces = calculateMuscleForces(gaitAnalysisResults);
```

Finite Element Analysis (FEA)

FINITE ELEMENT ANALYSIS is used to simulate the mechanical behavior of biological structures and tissues. MATLAB can be employed to create finite element models, solve them, and analyze the stress and strain within biological structures.

```
% Example of finite element analysis of bone structure

boneModel = createBoneModel(geometry, materialProperties);
```

```
boundaryConditions = specifyBoundaryConditions(boneModel);

loads = applyLoads(boneModel);

displacements = solveFEA(boneModel, boundaryConditions, loads);

stressStrainResults = analyzeStressStrain(displacements);
```

Muscle Simulation

SIMULATING MUSCLE BEHAVIOR is essential in biomechanics research. MATLAB can be used to model muscle activation, force generation, and muscle-tendon dynamics.

```
% Example of muscle activation and force generation simulation

muscleModel = createMuscleModel(muscleProperties);

activationSignal = generateActivationSignal();

forceGeneration = simulateMuscleForce(muscleModel, activationSignal);
```

Ergonomics and Human Factors

IN ERGONOMICS AND HUMAN factors studies, MATLAB can be employed to assess human interactions with products, environments, and workspaces. It helps in evaluating factors like reachability, posture, and biomechanical stress.

```
% Example of ergonomic analysis

workstationLayout = importWorkstationLayout('workstation_layout.xlsx');

reachabilityAnalysis = analyzeReachability(workstationLayout);
```

postureEvaluation = evaluatePosture(workstationLayout);

biomechanicalStress = assessBiomechanicalStress(workstationLayout);

Sports Biomechanics

SPORTS SCIENTISTS AND coaches often use MATLAB to analyze athletes' performance. It helps in understanding factors like sprint speed, jump height, and throwing mechanics.

% Example of sports biomechanics analysis

athleteData = loadAthletePerformanceData('athlete_performance.mat');

sprintSpeed = calculateSprintSpeed(athleteData);

jumpHeight = measureJumpPerformance(athleteData);

throwingMechanics = analyzeThrowingTechnique(athleteData);

Rehabilitation Engineering

REHABILITATION ENGINEERS use MATLAB to design assistive devices and technologies for individuals with disabilities. MATLAB facilitates the modeling of prosthetic limbs, exoskeletons, and other rehabilitation aids.

% Example of prosthetic limb modeling

prostheticModel = createProstheticLimbModel(physicalCharacteristics);

controlAlgorithm = designProstheticControl(prostheticModel);

simulateProstheticOperation(prostheticModel, controlAlgorithm);

In conclusion, MATLAB serves as a valuable tool for biomechanics and movement analysis in various fields, including sports science, rehabilitation engineering, ergonomics, and more. Researchers and professionals can leverage MATLAB's computational capabilities to gain insights into complex biomechanical phenomena, ultimately contributing to advancements in healthcare, sports performance, and human factors engineering.

Chapter 16: MATLAB in the Internet of Things (IoT)

Section 16.1: Connecting MATLAB to IoT Devices

IN THIS SECTION, WE will explore how MATLAB can be used to connect and interact with Internet of Things (IoT) devices. IoT has gained significant popularity in recent years due to its potential to connect everyday objects to the internet, enabling data collection, monitoring, and control from remote locations. MATLAB provides robust tools and capabilities to work with IoT devices, making it a valuable platform for IoT development.

Understanding IoT Devices:

IoT devices encompass a wide range of hardware, including sensors, actuators, microcontrollers, and more. These devices are typically equipped with the ability to collect data from their environment, process it, and communicate it over the internet or other networks.

Examples of IoT devices include temperature sensors, motion detectors, smart thermostats, and wearable fitness trackers.

Connecting MATLAB to IoT Devices:

MATLAB supports various communication protocols and interfaces to connect with IoT devices. You can use MATLAB to establish connections with IoT devices through Wi-Fi, Bluetooth, Ethernet, USB, and other communication channels. Additionally, MATLAB provides support for IoT-specific protocols such as MQTT (Message Queuing Telemetry Transport) and CoAP (Constrained Application Protocol).

% Example: Connecting to an IoT device over Wi-Fi

iotDevice = iot.Device('DeviceName', 'MyIoTDevice', 'Username', 'username', 'Password', 'password', 'BrokerURL', 'mqtt://broker.example.com');

Data Acquisition from IoT Devices:

Once connected, MATLAB allows you to collect data from IoT devices in real-time. You can create data acquisition scripts or applications to continuously retrieve sensor data from IoT devices. MATLAB's Data Acquisition Toolbox simplifies the process of reading data from sensors connected to your IoT device.

% Example: Reading temperature data from a connected IoT sensor

temperatureData = readSensorData(iotDevice, 'TemperatureSensor');

Analyzing IoT Data:

MATLAB's powerful data analysis and processing capabilities can be applied to the data collected from IoT devices. You can perform real-time analytics, apply machine learning algorithms, and visualize data trends to gain insights from IoT-generated data. This is particularly useful for applications like predictive maintenance and anomaly detection.

% Example: Real-time analysis of temperature data from IoT sensors

analyzeTemperatureData(temperatureData);

Control and Actuation:

In addition to data acquisition and analysis, MATLAB allows you to send commands and control actuators on IoT devices. This enables remote control and automation of IoT systems. You can create control algorithms and scripts to actuate devices based on predefined conditions or user inputs.

% Example: Sending a command to turn on an IoT-controlled light

sendCommand(iotDevice, 'LightControl', 'TurnOn');

Security and Authentication:

Security is a critical aspect of IoT applications. MATLAB provides mechanisms for secure communication with IoT devices. You can implement authentication, encryption, and secure protocols to protect data exchanged between MATLAB and IoT devices.

% Example: Implementing secure communication with IoT devices

configureSecurity(iotDevice, 'TLS');

In summary, MATLAB offers a comprehensive ecosystem for developing and deploying IoT applications. Whether you are working on home automation, industrial IoT, or environmental monitoring projects, MATLAB's capabilities for connecting, acquiring data from, and controlling IoT devices make it a valuable tool for IoT development and research.

Stay tuned for the subsequent sections in this chapter, where we will delve deeper into various aspects of IoT with MATLAB, including data analysis, predictive maintenance, and cloud integration.

Section 16.2: Data Acquisition from Sensors

IN THE PREVIOUS SECTION, we discussed connecting MATLAB to IoT devices and the importance of data acquisition. In this section, we will explore the process of acquiring data from sensors connected to IoT devices and how MATLAB simplifies this task.

Sensors in IoT:

IoT devices are equipped with various sensors that collect data from their surroundings. These sensors can measure a wide range of physical properties, such as temperature, humidity, pressure, light, motion, and more. The data collected by these sensors is essential for monitoring and making decisions in IoT applications.

Sensor Types:

IoT sensors come in many types and have specific characteristics. Some common types of IoT sensors include:

- **Temperature Sensors:** Measure ambient temperature.
- **Humidity Sensors:** Measure the level of moisture in the air.
- **Pressure Sensors:** Measure atmospheric pressure.

- **Proximity Sensors:** Detect the presence or absence of nearby objects.
- **Light Sensors:** Measure ambient light levels.
- **Accelerometers:** Measure acceleration or motion.
- **Magnetometers:** Measure magnetic fields.
- **Gyroscopes:** Measure orientation and rotation.

Connecting Sensors to IoT Devices:

Before acquiring data from sensors, you need to establish connections between these sensors and your IoT device. This often involves wiring the sensors to specific pins or ports on your IoT hardware. For wireless sensors, pairing or configuring them with the IoT device is necessary.

Reading Sensor Data with MATLAB:

MATLAB provides tools and functions for reading data from various types of sensors. The Data Acquisition Toolbox and Instrument Control Toolbox are commonly used to interface with sensors connected to IoT devices.

```
% Example: Reading temperature data from a connected sensor

temperatureSensor = connectSensor(iotDevice, 'TemperatureSensor');

temperatureData = readSensorData(temperatureSensor);
```

Data Preprocessing:

Once you have acquired data from sensors, it is essential to preprocess the data to ensure its quality and reliability. Data preprocessing may involve filtering out noise, removing outliers, and converting data units if necessary. MATLAB's data processing and analysis capabilities can be employed for these tasks.

```
% Example: Data preprocessing for temperature data

filteredData = preprocessTemperatureData(temperatureData);
```

Real-time Data Acquisition:

In many IoT applications, real-time data acquisition is crucial. MATLAB allows you to continuously acquire data from sensors in real-time, enabling you to monitor and react to changing conditions immediately.

```
% Example: Continuously acquire data in real-time from multiple sensors

while true

sensorData = readRealTimeSensorData(iotDevice, 'TemperatureSensor', 'PressureSensor');

processAndDisplayData(sensorData);

pause(1); % Pause for 1 second before the next reading

end
```

Logging and Storage:

To maintain a historical record of sensor data or for offline analysis, MATLAB can log and store acquired data in various formats, such as spreadsheets or databases. This facilitates data retrieval and analysis at a later time.

```
% Example: Log sensor data to a CSV file for future analysis
```

logSensorDataToFile(sensorData, 'sensor_data.csv');

In summary, data acquisition from sensors is a fundamental aspect of IoT applications, and MATLAB provides a comprehensive set of tools and functions to streamline this process. Whether you are working on a small-scale IoT project or a large-scale industrial application, MATLAB's capabilities can help you efficiently acquire, preprocess, and analyze sensor data for informed decision-making.

Section 16.3: Analyzing IoT Data

AFTER ACQUIRING DATA from sensors in IoT devices, the next crucial step is to analyze the collected data to gain insights, detect patterns, and make informed decisions. In this section, we will explore how MATLAB can be used for analyzing IoT data efficiently.

Data Exploration:

Before diving into complex analysis techniques, it's essential to get a clear understanding of the collected IoT data. MATLAB provides various tools for data exploration, including summary statistics, data visualization, and plotting.

% Example: Calculate summary statistics for temperature sensor data

meanTemperature = mean(temperatureData);

medianTemperature = median(temperatureData);

minTemperature = min(temperatureData);

maxTemperature = max(temperatureData);

Time-Series Analysis:

Many IoT data sources, such as sensors, generate time-series data. MATLAB has robust capabilities for time-series analysis, including trend analysis, seasonality detection, and forecasting. These techniques are valuable for predicting future trends or anomalies.

% Example: Perform time-series forecasting for sensor data

temperatureTimeSeries = timeseries(temperatureData, timestamps);

forecastModel = fitlm(temperatureTimeSeries, 'Temperature ~ Time');

forecastedTemperature = predict(forecastModel, futureTimestamps);

Machine Learning for Anomaly Detection:

IoT data often contains anomalies or outliers that may indicate system faults or unusual conditions. MATLAB's machine learning and statistical toolbox can be employed for anomaly detection, enabling you to automatically identify and flag abnormal data points.

% Example: Detect anomalies in sensor data using a machine learning model

anomalyDetector = fitAnomalyDetectionModel(sensorData);

anomalies = detectAnomalies(anomalyDetector, sensorData);

Pattern Recognition:

If your IoT data contains patterns or sequences, MATLAB's pattern recognition and signal processing tools can be used to detect and analyze these patterns. This is especially useful for applications like gesture recognition or pattern-based control.

% Example: Detect patterns in motion sensor data

motionPattern = detectMotionPattern(motionSensorData);

Data Fusion and Integration:

IoT applications often involve data from multiple sensors or sources. MATLAB allows you to integrate and fuse data from various sensors to create a comprehensive view of the system's behavior.

% Example: Fuse data from temperature, humidity, and pressure sensors

fusedData = fuseSensorData(temperatureData, humidityData, pressureData);

Visualization and Reporting:

Communicating the results of your IoT data analysis is essential. MATLAB provides extensive capabilities for creating interactive visualizations, generating reports, and sharing insights with stakeholders.

% Example: Create a dashboard with interactive IoT data visualizations

createIoTDashboard(temperatureData, humidityData, pressureData);

Automation and Alerts:

In some IoT applications, it's crucial to automate decision-making based on data analysis results. MATLAB can be integrated with IoT platforms to trigger actions, send alerts, or control devices based on predefined rules.

% Example: Set up automated alerts for temperature exceeding a threshold

```
if meanTemperature > thresholdTemperature

sendAlert('Temperature exceeds threshold.');

end
```

In conclusion, MATLAB is a powerful tool for analyzing IoT data, offering a wide range of techniques for data exploration, time-series analysis, anomaly detection, pattern recognition, and more. By leveraging MATLAB's capabilities, you can turn raw IoT sensor data into actionable insights, enabling better decision-making and optimization of IoT systems.

Section 16.4: Predictive Maintenance Using MATLAB

PREDICTIVE MAINTENANCE is a critical application of IoT data analysis that aims to predict when equipment or machinery is likely to fail so that maintenance can be performed just in time to prevent costly breakdowns. MATLAB offers a robust platform for implementing predictive maintenance strategies in IoT systems.

Data Collection and Preprocessing:

Predictive maintenance begins with data collection from sensors monitoring the equipment's condition. This data may include information about temperature, vibration, pressure, and other relevant parameters. In MATLAB, you can preprocess this data by cleaning, filtering, and aligning it for analysis.

```
% Example: Preprocessing temperature and vibration sensor data

cleanedTemperatureData = preprocessData(temperatureSensorData);
```

```
filteredVibrationData = applyFilter(vibrationSensorData);

alignedData = alignData(cleanedTemperatureData, filteredVibrationData);
```

Feature Engineering:

Feature engineering involves selecting and extracting relevant features from the IoT data that can be used to build predictive models. MATLAB provides various feature extraction techniques and tools to help engineers and data scientists create informative features.

```
% Example: Extracting statistical features from sensor data

temperatureFeatures = extractStatisticalFeatures(temperatureData);

vibrationFeatures = extractStatisticalFeatures(vibrationData);

combinedFeatures = [temperatureFeatures, vibrationFeatures];
```

Predictive Modeling:

MATLAB offers a wide range of machine learning and statistical modeling techniques to build predictive maintenance models. These models can be trained using historical data to predict equipment failures or maintenance needs.

```
% Example: Building a predictive maintenance model

trainingData = [combinedFeatures, failureLabels];

predictiveModel = trainPredictiveModel(trainingData);
```

Real-Time Monitoring:

Once the predictive maintenance model is trained, it can be deployed in real-time to monitor equipment health continuously.

MATLAB allows you to integrate the model with IoT devices and systems to provide timely alerts and notifications when maintenance is predicted to be required.

```
% Example: Real-time monitoring and alerting

while true

currentData = acquireLiveDataFromSensors();

features = extractFeatures(currentData);

predictedFailureProbability = predict(predictiveModel, features);

if predictedFailureProbability > threshold

sendMaintenanceAlert();

end

pause(interval);

end
```

Performance Evaluation:

It's essential to evaluate the performance of predictive maintenance models regularly. MATLAB provides tools for assessing the accuracy, precision, recall, and other metrics of the model's predictions. This helps in fine-tuning the model for better reliability.

```
% Example: Evaluating model performance

testData = [testFeatures, actualFailureLabels];

predictions = predict(predictiveModel, testFeatures);
```

evaluationMetrics = evaluatePredictiveModel(predictions, actualFailureLabels);

Maintenance Scheduling:

Based on the predictions and the urgency of required maintenance, MATLAB can assist in scheduling maintenance activities efficiently. Maintenance scheduling can optimize downtime and reduce costs while ensuring equipment reliability.

% Example: Optimizing maintenance schedules

plannedMaintenanceDates = optimizeMaintenanceSchedule(predictions, maintenanceWindow);

Continuous Improvement:

Predictive maintenance is an iterative process. MATLAB allows you to continuously collect new data, retrain models, and improve the accuracy of predictions over time. This ensures that maintenance strategies remain effective and up-to-date.

In summary, MATLAB is a versatile platform for implementing predictive maintenance strategies in IoT applications. Its capabilities for data preprocessing, feature engineering, predictive modeling, real-time monitoring, and performance evaluation make it a valuable tool for ensuring the reliability and longevity of equipment and machinery in various industrial settings.

Section 16.5: Cloud Integration and Data Storage Solutions

INTEGRATING MATLAB with cloud services and implementing data storage solutions is crucial when working with IoT applications. Cloud integration allows for scalable storage, easy data access, and collaboration among multiple stakeholders. In this section, we explore how MATLAB can be used to seamlessly connect with cloud platforms and store IoT data efficiently.

Connecting to Cloud Services:

MATLAB offers various tools and libraries for connecting to popular cloud platforms such as Amazon Web Services (AWS), Microsoft Azure, Google Cloud Platform (GCP), and more. These integrations enable you to securely upload, retrieve, and process data stored in the cloud.

```
% Example: Connecting to AWS S3 bucket

awsAccessKey = 'YOUR_ACCESS_KEY';

awsSecretKey = 'YOUR_SECRET_KEY';

s3BucketName = 'your-bucket-name';

s3Client = aws.s3.Client(awsAccessKey, awsSecretKey);

s3Object = getObject(s3Client, s3BucketName, 'data/sensor_readings.csv');

sensorData = readSensorDataFromObject(s3Object);
```

Uploading IoT Data to Cloud Storage:

IoT data generated from sensors can be directly uploaded to cloud storage. MATLAB simplifies this process by providing functions to upload data to cloud buckets or containers.

```
% Example: Uploading IoT data to Azure Blob Storage

azureStorageAccount = 'your-storage-account';

azureStorageKey = 'your-storage-key';
```

```
containerName = 'iot-data-container';

azureBlobClient = azure.storage.blob.BlobServiceClient(azureStorageAccount, azureStorageKey);

uploadSensorDataToBlob(azureBlobClient, containerName, 'sensor_readings.csv', sensorData);
```

Data Retrieval and Processing:

Once IoT data is stored in the cloud, MATLAB can retrieve and process it efficiently. Cloud storage solutions offer features like data versioning and access control, ensuring data integrity and security.

```
% Example: Retrieving IoT data from Google Cloud Storage

gcpProjectID = 'your-project-id';

gcpBucketName = 'your-bucket-name';

gcpObject = gcp.storage.Object(gcpBucketName, 'data/sensor_readings.csv', 'project', gcpProjectID);

downloadedData = readSensorDataFromGCPObject(gcpObject);
```

Real-Time Analytics and Reporting:

MATLAB's analytical capabilities can be leveraged in the cloud to perform real-time data analysis and generate reports or visualizations. This is especially valuable for IoT applications where quick insights are essential.

```
% Example: Real-time analytics in MATLAB Online

cloudMATLAB = matlab.online.Session.getInstance();

realTimeAnalyticsScript = 'analyze_sensor_data.m';
```

runScriptInCloud(cloudMATLAB, realTimeAnalyticsScript);

Collaborative Workspaces:

MATLAB Online and cloud-based services allow multiple users to collaborate on IoT projects simultaneously. Shared workspaces and project management tools enable effective teamwork and knowledge sharing.

% Example: Collaborative workspace in MATLAB Online

collaboratorEmail = 'collaborator@example.com';

inviteToWorkspace(cloudMATLAB, collaboratorEmail);

Scalability and Resource Management:

Cloud integration in MATLAB offers scalability by dynamically allocating computational resources as needed. This ensures that IoT applications can handle growing data volumes and computational demands effectively.

% Example: Scaling IoT data processing in AWS Lambda

awsLambdaFunction = 'your-lambda-function';

awsLambdaClient = aws.lambda.LambdaClient(awsAccessKey, awsSecretKey);

invokeLambdaFunction(awsLambdaClient, awsLambdaFunction, sensorData);

Data Archiving and Backup:

Cloud platforms provide robust data archiving and backup solutions. MATLAB can automate the process of archiving historical IoT data, ensuring data availability and redundancy.

```
% Example: Automated data archiving in Azure Archive Storage

archiveStorageAccount = 'your-archive-account';

archiveStorageKey = 'your-archive-key';

archiveContainerName = 'archive-data-container';

archiveSensorDataToBlob(azureBlobClient, archiveContainerName, 'sensor_readings_2023.csv', historicalData);
```

In conclusion, integrating MATLAB with cloud services and utilizing cloud-based data storage solutions is essential for managing IoT data effectively. Whether you're working with sensor data, analytics, or collaborative projects, MATLAB provides the tools and flexibility to streamline your IoT workflow and take full advantage of the cloud's capabilities. This integration ensures that IoT applications can scale, remain secure, and operate efficiently in a cloud-centric world.

Chapter 17: High-Performance Computing with MATLAB

Section 17.1: Parallel Computing in MATLAB

PARALLEL COMPUTING is a powerful technique that allows you to leverage multiple CPU cores or even distributed computing resources to perform tasks concurrently. MATLAB provides extensive support for parallel computing, making it possible to speed up computationally intensive tasks and significantly reduce processing times.

Benefits of Parallel Computing in MATLAB

1. **Faster Execution**: One of the primary advantages of parallel computing is that it allows you to execute your MATLAB code much faster. By distributing tasks across multiple cores or nodes, you can achieve significant speed improvements for computationally demanding operations.
2. **Efficient Resource Utilization**: MATLAB's parallel computing capabilities enable efficient utilization of available resources, whether you have a multi-core CPU or access to a cluster of machines. This can result in better resource management and reduced waiting times for your computations.
3. **Scalability**: Parallel computing in MATLAB is scalable, meaning it can be applied to a wide range of problems, from small-scale parallelism on a single machine to large-scale distributed computing across a cluster or the cloud.
4. **Improved Productivity**: Faster computation times mean quicker results and increased productivity. Parallel

computing is particularly beneficial for engineers, scientists, and researchers who deal with simulations, data analysis, and optimization.

Types of Parallelism in MATLAB

MATLAB OFFERS SEVERAL approaches to parallel computing:

1. **Multi-Core Parallelism**: This involves utilizing the multiple CPU cores available on a single machine. MATLAB's Parallel Computing Toolbox provides functions like parfor (parallel for loops) and parpool to distribute tasks across these cores.
2. **GPU Acceleration**: MATLAB can harness the computational power of Graphics Processing Units (GPUs) for certain tasks. The Parallel Computing Toolbox includes GPU support for accelerating specific operations, such as deep learning and numerical simulations.
3. **Cluster Computing**: For even more significant parallelism, you can set up a cluster of machines and distribute tasks across them using MATLAB Distributed Computing Server. This approach is suitable for tackling large-scale simulations or data processing tasks.

Example of Multi-Core Parallelism in MATLAB

HERE'S A SIMPLE EXAMPLE demonstrating the use of parfor for multi-core parallelism in MATLAB:

% Define a range of values to process in parallel

valuesToProcess = 1:1000;

% Create a parallel pool with multiple workers (CPU cores)

```
pool = parpool('local', 4); % Create a pool with 4 workers
% Perform a computationally intensive operation in parallel
result = zeros(size(valuesToProcess));
parfor i = 1:length(valuesToProcess)
result(i) = myFunction(valuesToProcess(i)); % Your custom function
end
% Close the parallel pool
delete(pool);
```

In this example, parfor distributes the iterations of the loop across multiple workers in the parallel pool, allowing for concurrent execution and faster results.

In summary, parallel computing in MATLAB offers substantial performance improvements by leveraging the capabilities of modern hardware. Whether you're working on complex simulations, data analysis, or machine learning tasks, understanding and utilizing parallelism can significantly enhance your MATLAB workflow and reduce computation times. This section will explore various aspects of parallel computing in MATLAB, including multi-core parallelism, GPU acceleration, and distributed computing across clusters.

Section 17.2: GPU Acceleration Techniques in MATLAB

GRAPHICS PROCESSING Units (GPUs) have become an integral part of high-performance computing, capable of accelerating various types of computations. MATLAB provides robust support for GPU acceleration, allowing you to harness the computational power of GPUs for specific tasks. In this section, we'll explore GPU acceleration techniques in MATLAB and discuss scenarios where it can be advantageous.

Benefits of GPU Acceleration

GPU ACCELERATION OFFERS several benefits when compared to traditional CPU-based computations:

1. **Speed**: GPUs are designed for parallelism and can perform thousands of mathematical operations simultaneously. This leads to significant speed improvements for tasks that can be parallelized.
2. **Large-Scale Data**: GPUs have large memory bandwidth and can efficiently handle large datasets, making them ideal for tasks involving extensive data processing.
3. **Deep Learning**: Deep learning, a subset of machine learning, often involves training complex neural networks with many layers. GPUs excel at accelerating deep learning tasks, reducing training times from days to hours or even minutes.
4. **Scientific Computing**: Complex scientific simulations, such as fluid dynamics or molecular modeling, benefit from GPU acceleration due to the ability to parallelize computations.

GPU Support in MATLAB

MATLAB'S GPU SUPPORT is primarily provided through the Parallel Computing Toolbox and the MATLAB Deep Learning Toolbox. Here's an overview of how to leverage GPUs in MATLAB:

1. **GPU Arrays**: MATLAB allows you to create GPU arrays,

which are data structures similar to regular arrays but reside in GPU memory. You can perform operations on GPU arrays using MATLAB functions, and MATLAB automatically manages data transfer between CPU and GPU.

2. **Deep Learning**: MATLAB's Deep Learning Toolbox includes GPU support for training and deploying deep neural networks. Popular deep learning frameworks like TensorFlow and PyTorch also integrate with MATLAB's GPU capabilities.
3. **GPU Functions**: MATLAB provides GPU-enabled versions of many built-in functions, making it easy to accelerate computations. For example, gpuArray converts data to GPU arrays, and functions like gpuFFT and gpuSVD perform GPU-accelerated fast Fourier transforms and singular value decompositions.

Example of GPU Acceleration in MATLAB

LET'S CONSIDER A SIMPLE example of performing matrix multiplication using GPU acceleration in MATLAB:

% Create random matrices on the CPU

A = rand(1000, 1000);

B = rand(1000, 1000);

% Transfer matrices to the GPU

A_gpu = gpuArray(A);

B_gpu = gpuArray(B);

% Perform matrix multiplication on the GPU

```
C_gpu = A_gpu * B_gpu;

% Transfer the result back to the CPU

C = gather(C_gpu);
```

In this example, gpuArray is used to transfer matrices to the GPU, and the matrix multiplication is performed on the GPU. The gather function is then used to bring the result back to the CPU.

When to Use GPU Acceleration

GPU ACCELERATION IS most beneficial when dealing with computationally intensive tasks that can be parallelized. Here are some scenarios where GPU acceleration is valuable:

- Training deep neural networks for machine learning tasks.
- Large-scale numerical simulations, such as finite element analysis or computational fluid dynamics.
- Cryptographic operations, including hashing and encryption.
- Image and video processing tasks, such as real-time video enhancement or computer vision.
- Complex mathematical operations, such as large matrix computations.

In summary, GPU acceleration in MATLAB offers a powerful way to speed up specific computations and tackle tasks that require significant parallel processing. By utilizing GPU arrays and GPU-enabled functions, you can take advantage of the computational capabilities of modern GPUs to enhance the performance of your MATLAB applications.

Section 17.3: Large-Scale Data Handling in MATLAB

HANDLING LARGE-SCALE datasets efficiently is a crucial aspect of scientific computing and data analysis. MATLAB provides a range of techniques and tools to work with big data, allowing you to process, analyze, and visualize extensive datasets. In this section, we'll explore various approaches to handle large-scale data in MATLAB.

1. Tall Arrays

MATLAB INTRODUCED TALL Arrays as part of the Parallel Computing Toolbox. Tall Arrays are a convenient way to work with data that doesn't fit into memory. They allow you to perform operations on data that is too large to load entirely into RAM by dividing it into smaller "chunks" that can be processed sequentially. This approach enables you to work with data that exceeds your system's memory capacity.

```
% Create a tall array from a data source (e.g., a big CSV file)

data = tall(readtable('large_data.csv'));

% Perform operations on the tall array

result = data.groupBy('Category').sum('Value');
```

2. Datastore and Parallel Computing

MATLAB PROVIDES THE Datastore framework, which allows you to work with large data sources, such as databases, Hadoop

Distributed File System (HDFS), or cloud storage, without loading the entire dataset into memory. You can use Parallel Computing Toolbox functions to process data in parallel, making efficient use of multi-core CPUs.

```
% Create a Datastore for a large file

ds = datastore('big_data.csv');

% Process data in parallel

parfor i = 1:length(ds.Files)

data = read(ds);

% Perform operations on data

end
```

3. Database Connectivity

IF YOUR LARGE-SCALE data is stored in a database, MATLAB provides database connectivity tools to query and analyze data directly from the database. You can use functions like database, exec, and fetch to interact with databases.

```
% Connect to a database

conn = database('mydb', 'username', 'password');

% Execute SQL queries

query = 'SELECT * FROM large_table';

data = fetch(conn, query);

% Analyze and visualize data in MATLAB
```

4. Memory-Mapped Files

MEMORY-MAPPED FILES enable you to work with data that is too large to fit in memory. MATLAB allows you to create a memory-mapped file object that represents a file on disk and map parts of it into memory as needed.

```
% Create a memory-mapped file

filename = 'large_data.bin';

mmf = memmapfile(filename, 'Format', 'double');

% Access and manipulate data in chunks

chunkSize = 10000;

for i = 1:chunkSize:length(mmf.Data)

dataChunk = mmf.Data(i:min(i+chunkSize-1, end));

% Perform operations on the chunk

end
```

5. Distributed Computing

FOR EXTREMELY LARGE datasets and computationally intensive tasks, you can take advantage of distributed computing capabilities in MATLAB. The Parallel Computing Toolbox enables you to distribute computations across multiple CPUs or even clusters of machines.

```
% Create a parallel pool of workers

pool = parpool('local', 4);

% Distribute computations across workers
```

spmd

% Your parallel code here

end

% Retrieve and consolidate results

In summary, MATLAB offers a range of tools and techniques to handle large-scale data efficiently. Whether you're dealing with tall arrays, datastores, database connectivity, memory-mapped files, or distributed computing, MATLAB provides the flexibility and scalability to process and analyze massive datasets, making it a valuable tool for data scientists and researchers working with big data.

Section 17.4: Distributed Computing and MATLAB

DISTRIBUTED COMPUTING is a powerful technique that allows you to leverage multiple computing resources, such as multi-core processors or even clusters of machines, to speed up computations and handle large-scale data. MATLAB provides robust support for distributed computing through the Parallel Computing Toolbox. In this section, we will explore how to harness the capabilities of distributed computing in MATLAB.

1. Parallel Computing Toolbox

THE PARALLEL COMPUTING Toolbox extends MATLAB's capabilities to work with parallel and distributed computing resources. It allows you to distribute your computations across multiple cores or workers, making it especially valuable for tasks that require significant computational resources.

Parallel Pool Creation

TO GET STARTED WITH distributed computing, you can create a parallel pool of workers. A worker is a separate MATLAB session that can execute tasks in parallel.

```
% Create a parallel pool with a specific number of workers

pool = parpool('local', 4); % Creates a pool with 4 workers
```

Parallel Computing Constructs

MATLAB OFFERS CONSTRUCTS like parfor (parallel for loop) and spmd (single program, multiple data) to parallelize your code. These constructs distribute tasks to workers, allowing for parallel execution.

```
% Example of using parfor for parallel execution

parfor i = 1:100

% Your parallel code here

end

% Example of using spmd to create parallel code blocks

spmd

% Your parallel code here

end
```

2. Parallel Data Processing

WITH DISTRIBUTED COMPUTING, you can process large datasets in parallel. For instance, you can divide a dataset into chunks and assign each chunk to a different worker for simultaneous processing.

```
% Divide a large dataset into chunks

data = rand(10000, 10000);

chunkSize = size(data, 1) / numWorkers;

% Parallel processing using parfor

parfor i = 1:numWorkers

startIndex = (i - 1) * chunkSize + 1;

endIndex = i * chunkSize;

chunk = data(startIndex:endIndex, :);

% Process the chunk in parallel

end
```

3. Distributed Computing on Clusters

MATLAB'S PARALLEL COMPUTING Toolbox also supports cluster computing. You can set up a cluster of machines and distribute your computations across them for even greater parallelism.

```
% Connect to a cluster profile (if configured)

cluster = parcluster('MyClusterProfile');

% Create a parallel pool on the cluster

pool = parpool(cluster, numWorkers);
```

4. Task Synchronization

SYNCHRONIZING TASKS and collecting results from workers is essential. MATLAB provides functions like fetchOutputs, parfeval, and fetchNext to manage tasks and gather results efficiently.

```
% Perform computations asynchronously and collect results

results = cell(1, numTasks);

for i = 1:numTasks

results{i} = parfeval(pool, @yourFunction, 1, args{i});

end

% Collect results as they become available

for i = 1:numTasks

[completedIdx, result] = fetchNext(results);

% Process the result

end
```

5. Scaling and Load Balancing

YOU CAN DYNAMICALLY adjust the number of workers or machines in the cluster to optimize resource utilization and achieve load balancing for your computations.

```
% Dynamically adjust the number of workers

pool = gcp('nocreate'); % Get the current pool if it exists

if isempty(pool) || pool.NumWorkers ~= newNumWorkers

delete(pool); % Close the current pool if it exists
```

```
pool = parpool('local', newNumWorkers); % Create a new pool
end
```

In conclusion, MATLAB's Parallel Computing Toolbox empowers you to distribute and parallelize your computations, making it easier to tackle large-scale data and compute-intensive tasks. Whether you're working on a multi-core machine or a cluster, MATLAB's support for distributed computing allows you to harness the full potential of your computational resources efficiently.

Section 17.5: Performance Optimization Strategies

EFFICIENTLY OPTIMIZING your MATLAB code can lead to substantial improvements in execution speed and resource utilization. In this section, we'll explore various performance optimization strategies that can help you achieve better results.

1. Vectorization

ONE OF THE FUNDAMENTAL principles of MATLAB optimization is vectorization. MATLAB is designed to perform operations on entire arrays efficiently. By vectorizing your code and avoiding explicit loops, you can significantly improve performance.

```
% Non-vectorized approach
result = zeros(1, 1000);
for i = 1:1000
result(i) = x(i) * y(i);
end
```

```
% Vectorized approach (faster)

result = x .* y;
```

2. Preallocation

WHEN WORKING WITH ARRAYS that will grow in size during execution, preallocating memory for those arrays can prevent MATLAB from repeatedly resizing them, which is computationally expensive.

```
% Non-preallocated array (inefficient)

result = [];

for i = 1:1000

result(i) = someFunction(i);

end

% Preallocated array (faster)

result = zeros(1, 1000);

for i = 1:1000

result(i) = someFunction(i);

end
```

3. Memory Management

EFFICIENT MEMORY MANAGEMENT can have a significant impact on performance. Avoid creating unnecessary variables or copies of data when not needed. Clear variables you no longer use to free up memory.

```
% Inefficient memory usage
a = rand(1000);
b = a; % Creates a copy of 'a'
% Efficient memory usage
a = rand(1000);
clear b; % Clears 'b' when it's no longer needed
```

4. Algorithm Selection

CHOOSING THE RIGHT algorithm for your task is crucial. Some algorithms are more efficient for specific operations than others. MATLAB provides various built-in functions and toolboxes optimized for specific tasks.

```
% Inefficient sorting
sortedArray = sort(unsortedArray);
% Efficient sorting (built-in)
sortedArray = sort(unsortedArray, 'ascend');
```

5. Parallel Computing

AS DISCUSSED IN PREVIOUS sections, parallel computing can significantly boost performance for computationally intensive tasks. Utilize MATLAB's Parallel Computing Toolbox to distribute computations across multiple cores or machines.

```
% Parallel computing for a time-consuming task
parfor i = 1:numTasks
```

```
result(i) = computeTask(i);
end
```

6. Profiling and Benchmarking

MATLAB PROVIDES PROFILING tools that help you identify performance bottlenecks in your code. Use the Profiler to pinpoint functions or lines of code that consume the most time or resources.

```
% Profile your code
profile on;
yourFunction();
profile off;
% Analyze the profiling results
profilerViewer;
```

7. Mex Files

FOR COMPUTATIONALLY intensive tasks, consider creating MEX files by compiling C/C++ code into MATLAB executables. This can result in significant performance gains.

```
% Create a MEX file from C/C++ code
mex yourFunction.c
```

8. Optimized Libraries and Toolboxes

EXPLORE MATLAB'S OPTIMIZED libraries and toolboxes for specific tasks. These libraries are often finely tuned for high performance.

```
% Utilize specialized toolboxes

result = specializedFunction(inputData);
```

9. Hardware Acceleration

LEVERAGE HARDWARE ACCELERATION, such as GPU computing, when applicable. MATLAB supports GPU acceleration for various operations, especially in deep learning and numerical computing.

```
% Utilize GPU for matrix operations

gpuArrayA = gpuArray(A);

gpuArrayB = gpuArray(B);

result = gpuArrayA * gpuArrayB;
```

10. Code Review and Optimization

LASTLY, CONSIDER HAVING your code reviewed by peers or experts. Sometimes, a fresh perspective can lead to optimization ideas that you might have missed.

In conclusion, optimizing MATLAB code is a crucial step in achieving better performance and making the most of computational resources. By following these optimization strategies, you can enhance the efficiency of your code and reduce execution times, ultimately leading to more productive and effective MATLAB programming.

Chapter 18: Case Studies and Real-World Applications

Section 18.1: Case Study: Environmental Monitoring System

IN THIS SECTION, WE'LL explore a real-world case study that demonstrates how MATLAB can be used to develop an environmental monitoring system. Such systems are crucial for collecting and analyzing data related to environmental parameters like air quality, temperature, humidity, and more.

Introduction

ENVIRONMENTAL MONITORING systems play a vital role in modern society, helping us track and manage various environmental factors. They are used in urban planning, agriculture, industrial processes, and more. Our case study focuses on developing a MATLAB-based environmental monitoring system for air quality.

Problem Statement

IMAGINE WE WANT TO create a system that monitors air quality in an urban area and provides real-time data on pollutant levels, temperature, and humidity. Additionally, the system should generate alerts when pollutant levels exceed predefined thresholds.

MATLAB Implementation

HERE'S AN OUTLINE OF how we can implement this system using MATLAB:

1. **Data Acquisition**: Use sensors to collect data on air

quality, temperature, and humidity. These sensors may be connected to a microcontroller or IoT device.

2. **Data Processing**: Read data from sensors and preprocess it. This may involve data cleaning, calibration, and noise reduction.
3. **Threshold Monitoring**: Define threshold levels for pollutants. Create algorithms to compare real-time data with these thresholds.
4. **Alert Generation**: If pollutant levels exceed the thresholds, trigger alerts. This can be done through notifications, emails, or visual indicators.
5. **Data Storage**: Store the collected data in a database for historical analysis and reporting.
6. **Visualization**: Create MATLAB plots and graphs to visualize real-time and historical data trends. This helps in understanding air quality variations over time.
7. **Reporting**: Generate reports summarizing air quality statistics and trends. These reports can be automatically generated and sent to relevant authorities or stakeholders.

```
% Sample MATLAB code for reading sensor data

sensorData = readSensorData();

% Preprocess the data (e.g., calibration, noise reduction)

% Define pollutant thresholds

thresholds = struct('CO2', 1000, 'NO2', 50, 'PM2.5', 10);

% Check if pollutant levels exceed thresholds

exceededThresholds = checkThresholds(sensorData, thresholds);

if any(exceededThresholds)
```

```
% Trigger alerts and notifications
sendAlerts();
end
% Store data in a database
storeData(sensorData);
% Visualize data using MATLAB plots
plotData(sensorData);
% Generate and send reports
generateReports(sensorData);
```

Benefits

DEVELOPING SUCH AN environmental monitoring system in MATLAB offers several advantages:

- **Rapid Prototyping**: MATLAB's ease of use and extensive toolboxes allow for quick prototyping and testing of algorithms.
- **Data Analysis**: MATLAB's powerful data analysis and visualization capabilities make it suitable for understanding complex environmental data.
- **Integration**: MATLAB supports integration with IoT devices and databases, making it versatile for real-world applications.

- **Customization**: MATLAB allows developers to customize algorithms and alerts based on specific environmental needs.

Conclusion

THIS CASE STUDY DEMONSTRATES how MATLAB can be used to develop an environmental monitoring system. Similar approaches can be applied to various real-world applications, showcasing MATLAB's versatility and effectiveness in solving complex problems.

Section 18.2: Case Study: Financial Forecasting Model

IN THIS SECTION, WE will delve into a real-world case study that highlights the use of MATLAB in developing a financial forecasting model. Financial forecasting is a critical aspect of decision-making in various industries, including finance, investment, and business management.

Introduction

FINANCIAL FORECASTING involves predicting future financial outcomes based on historical data, market trends, and other relevant factors. A well-designed forecasting model can help organizations make informed decisions about budgeting, investment, and risk management. Our case study focuses on building a MATLAB-based financial forecasting model for a hypothetical investment portfolio.

Problem Statement

IMAGINE YOU ARE AN investment manager responsible for a portfolio of stocks and bonds. Your goal is to create a forecasting model that can predict the portfolio's future performance based on historical data, economic indicators, and market sentiment. Additionally, you want to assess the impact of various economic scenarios on the portfolio's returns.

MATLAB Implementation

HERE'S AN OUTLINE OF how we can implement this financial forecasting model using MATLAB:

1. **Data Collection**: Gather historical data for the portfolio, including stock prices, bond yields, and economic indicators. MATLAB provides tools for importing and managing financial data.
2. **Data Preprocessing**: Clean and preprocess the data, handling missing values and outliers. Normalize the data if necessary.
3. **Feature Selection**: Identify relevant features that may impact the portfolio's performance, such as GDP growth, interest rates, and inflation.
4. **Model Building**: Choose an appropriate forecasting model. MATLAB offers various modeling techniques, including time series analysis, regression, and machine learning.
5. **Model Training**: Train the selected model using historical data. Adjust model parameters and hyperparameters for optimal performance.
6. **Scenario Analysis**: Use the trained model to perform scenario analysis. For example, assess how the portfolio

would perform under different economic conditions (e.g., recession, growth).

7. **Visualization**: Create MATLAB visualizations, such as time series plots, risk-reward profiles, and sensitivity analyses, to understand and communicate the forecasted results.

```
% Sample MATLAB code for financial forecasting

% Import historical data

portfolioData = importFinancialData('portfolio.csv');

% Data preprocessing

cleanedData = preprocessData(portfolioData);

% Feature selection (select relevant economic indicators)

selectedFeatures = selectFeatures(cleanedData);

% Choose a forecasting model (e.g., ARIMA, LSTM)

model = trainForecastingModel(selectedFeatures);

% Perform scenario analysis

economicScenarios = generateScenarios();

scenarioResults = assessScenarios(model, economicScenarios);

% Visualize forecasted results

plotResults(scenarioResults);
```

Benefits

DEVELOPING A FINANCIAL forecasting model in MATLAB offers several advantages:

- **Data Handling**: MATLAB provides extensive tools for importing, cleaning, and managing financial data.
- **Modeling Flexibility**: MATLAB's modeling capabilities allow for the implementation of various forecasting techniques, from traditional time series analysis to advanced machine learning models.
- **Visualization**: MATLAB's visualization capabilities help in presenting forecasted results effectively.
- **Scenario Analysis**: The ability to perform scenario analysis is crucial for understanding the portfolio's sensitivity to economic conditions.

Conclusion

THIS CASE STUDY ILLUSTRATES how MATLAB can be employed to build a financial forecasting model for investment portfolios. The flexibility, data handling, and visualization capabilities of MATLAB make it a powerful tool for financial analysts and decision-makers in the finance industry.

Section 18.3: Case Study: Autonomous Vehicle Algorithms

IN THIS SECTION, WE will explore a real-world case study that demonstrates the application of MATLAB in developing algorithms for autonomous vehicles. Autonomous vehicles, also known as self-driving cars, are a transformative technology with applications in transportation, logistics, and mobility services.

Introduction

THE DEVELOPMENT OF autonomous vehicles requires sophisticated algorithms for perception, control, and decision-making. MATLAB provides a comprehensive environment for prototyping, testing, and deploying these algorithms.

Problem Statement

IMAGINE YOU ARE PART of a team tasked with developing algorithms for an autonomous vehicle. The vehicle needs to navigate city streets, detect and respond to traffic signals, pedestrians, and other vehicles, and make decisions to ensure safe and efficient travel. Your goal is to use MATLAB to develop and test these algorithms.

MATLAB Implementation

HERE'S AN OUTLINE OF how MATLAB can be utilized in the development of autonomous vehicle algorithms:

1. **Simulated Environment**: Create a simulated environment within MATLAB where the autonomous vehicle can operate. MATLAB's Simulink tool is particularly useful for this purpose.
2. **Sensor Modeling**: Develop models for various sensors used by the vehicle, such as LiDAR, cameras, and radar. MATLAB provides tools for sensor modeling and simulation.
3. **Perception Algorithms**: Implement perception algorithms to process sensor data and identify objects in the vehicle's surroundings. This may involve computer vision and

machine learning techniques.

4. **Control Algorithms**: Develop control algorithms that enable the vehicle to follow a desired path, adjust its speed, and respond to dynamic obstacles and traffic conditions.
5. **Decision-Making**: Implement decision-making algorithms that consider the vehicle's current state, sensor inputs, and traffic rules to make safe and efficient driving decisions.
6. **Simulation and Testing**: Use MATLAB's simulation capabilities to test the algorithms in a virtual environment, simulating various driving scenarios and edge cases.
7. **Hardware Integration**: Once the algorithms are validated in simulation, they can be integrated with the vehicle's hardware for real-world testing and deployment.

```
% Sample MATLAB code for autonomous vehicle algorithm development

% Create a simulated environment

simEnv = createSimulationEnvironment('cityscape');

% Sensor modeling

lidarModel = createLiDARModel();

cameraModel = createCameraModel();

radarModel = createRadarModel();

% Perception algorithms (object detection and tracking)

objectDetector = trainObjectDetector(trainingData);

objectTracker = createObjectTracker();
```

```
% Control algorithms (path planning and speed control)

pathPlanner = createPathPlanner();

speedController = createSpeedController();

% Decision-making algorithm (rule-based or machine learning-based)

decisionMaker = createDecisionMaker();

% Simulation and testing

simulatedCar = initializeSimulatedVehicle();

simulatedCar.addSensor(lidarModel);

simulatedCar.addSensor(cameraModel);

simulatedCar.addSensor(radarModel);

% Loop through simulated scenarios

for scenario = simulatedScenarios

sensorData = simulatedCar.captureSensorData();

detectedObjects = objectDetector(sensorData);

trackedObjects = objectTracker(detectedObjects);

plannedPath = pathPlanner(trackedObjects);

desiredSpeed = speedController(trackedObjects, plannedPath);

drivingDecision = decisionMaker(sensorData, plannedPath, desiredSpeed);

simulatedCar.updateState(drivingDecision);

end
```

Benefits

DEVELOPING AUTONOMOUS vehicle algorithms in MATLAB offers several benefits:

- **Simulation Environment**: MATLAB's simulation tools provide a safe and cost-effective environment for algorithm development and testing.
- **Sensor Modeling**: MATLAB allows for the modeling and testing of sensors in various conditions.
- **Algorithm Integration**: MATLAB's modular approach facilitates the integration of perception, control, and decision-making algorithms.
- **Scenario Testing**: MATLAB enables testing in diverse driving scenarios, including rare and challenging situations.
- **Hardware Deployment**: Once validated, MATLAB algorithms can be deployed to real-world vehicles.

Conclusion

THIS CASE STUDY SHOWCASES the versatility of MATLAB in developing algorithms for autonomous vehicles. The combination of simulation, sensor modeling, and algorithm development tools in MATLAB makes it a valuable platform for engineers and researchers working in the field of autonomous transportation.

Section 18.4: Case Study: Medical Diagnostic Software

IN THIS SECTION, WE delve into a real-world case study that illustrates the development of medical diagnostic software using MATLAB. MATLAB's computational capabilities and extensive toolbox support make it an ideal choice for creating software that aids in medical diagnosis and decision-making.

Introduction

MEDICAL DIAGNOSTIC software plays a crucial role in assisting healthcare professionals in making accurate diagnoses, analyzing medical images, and interpreting patient data. In this case study, we will focus on the development of software for the early detection of a specific medical condition, leveraging MATLAB's capabilities.

Problem Statement

IMAGINE YOU ARE PART of a team tasked with developing diagnostic software to assist radiologists in the early detection of breast cancer using mammogram images. The goal is to create a software tool that can analyze mammogram images, identify potential abnormalities, and provide diagnostic insights.

MATLAB Implementation

HERE'S HOW MATLAB CAN be utilized in the development of medical diagnostic software for breast cancer detection:

1. **Data Collection and Preprocessing**: Gather a dataset of mammogram images, ensuring it is properly labeled. Use MATLAB to preprocess and augment the data, such as resizing images, enhancing contrast, and normalizing pixel

values.

2. **Image Segmentation**: Implement image segmentation algorithms to identify regions of interest within mammogram images. MATLAB's Image Processing Toolbox provides a wide range of tools for this purpose.
3. **Feature Extraction**: Extract relevant features from segmented regions to characterize potential abnormalities. Features may include texture, shape, and intensity descriptors. MATLAB offers functions for feature extraction and selection.
4. **Machine Learning Models**: Train machine learning models, such as support vector machines (SVMs) or convolutional neural networks (CNNs), using the extracted features and labeled data. MATLAB's Machine Learning Toolbox simplifies model training and evaluation.
5. **Diagnostic Decision**: Develop algorithms that use the trained model to make diagnostic decisions based on input mammogram images. This step involves thresholding or probability estimation.
6. **User Interface**: Create a user-friendly graphical user interface (GUI) using MATLAB's App Designer or GUIDE to allow radiologists to interact with the software, upload mammogram images, and view diagnostic results.
7. **Validation and Testing**: Thoroughly validate the software using a diverse dataset, including cases with known outcomes. Assess the software's sensitivity, specificity, and accuracy.

% Sample MATLAB code for medical diagnostic software

% Data preprocessing

```
data = preprocessMammogramData('mammogram_dataset');

% Image segmentation

segmentedImages = segmentMammograms(data);

% Feature extraction

features = extractFeatures(segmentedImages);

% Machine learning model training (SVM as an example)

svmModel = fitSVM(features, data.labels);

% Diagnostic decision

testImage = loadMammogram('test_image.png');

featuresTest = extractFeatures(segmentMammogram(testImage));

predictedLabel = predict(svmModel, featuresTest);

% User interface (GUI)

app = diagnosticApp();

app.UIFigure.Visible = 'on';

% Validation and testing

accuracy = assessModelPerformance(svmModel, testData);
```

Benefits

DEVELOPING MEDICAL diagnostic software with MATLAB offers several advantages:

- **Data Preprocessing**: MATLAB provides tools for efficient data preprocessing and augmentation.

- **Image Processing**: MATLAB's Image Processing Toolbox simplifies image segmentation and feature extraction.

- **Machine Learning**: MATLAB's Machine Learning Toolbox offers a wide range of algorithms for model training.

- **User Interface**: MATLAB's GUI development tools enable the creation of intuitive interfaces for healthcare professionals.

- **Validation**: MATLAB allows for rigorous validation and testing of the diagnostic software's performance.

Conclusion

THIS CASE STUDY SHOWCASES how MATLAB can be applied to develop medical diagnostic software, specifically for early breast cancer detection. MATLAB's capabilities in image processing, machine learning, and GUI development make it a valuable platform for creating powerful and accurate diagnostic tools to aid healthcare professionals in their work.

Section 18.5: Case Study: Smart Grid Energy Analysis

IN THIS SECTION, WE explore a real-world case study that focuses on the application of MATLAB in analyzing and optimizing energy consumption in a smart grid. Smart grids are modern electrical grids that utilize advanced technologies to improve efficiency, reliability, and sustainability.

Introduction

SMART GRIDS ARE AN essential component of the transition to clean and efficient energy systems. They integrate renewable energy sources, such as solar and wind, and employ advanced monitoring and control systems to balance supply and demand. MATLAB provides powerful tools for modeling, simulating, and optimizing smart grid operations.

Problem Statement

IMAGINE YOU ARE PART of a team tasked with optimizing the operation of a smart grid serving a metropolitan area. The goal is to minimize energy losses, reduce peak demand, and integrate renewable energy sources effectively while ensuring grid stability and reliability.

MATLAB Implementation

HERE'S HOW MATLAB CAN be applied to address the challenges in optimizing a smart grid:

1. **Data Acquisition**: MATLAB can interface with sensors and data sources to collect real-time data on energy consumption, weather conditions, and renewable energy generation.
2. **Load Forecasting**: Develop machine learning models to forecast energy demand accurately. MATLAB's Machine Learning Toolbox can be used for time series forecasting.
3. **Renewable Energy Integration**: Optimize the integration of renewable energy sources by modeling solar and wind power generation. MATLAB provides tools for simulating and analyzing renewable energy systems.
4. **Energy Storage Optimization**: Design and implement

energy storage solutions like batteries and supercapacitors. MATLAB helps in modeling and optimizing energy storage systems.

5. **Grid Control and Management**: Develop control algorithms to manage grid operations efficiently. MATLAB supports control system design and simulation.
6. **Stability Analysis**: Analyze grid stability using MATLAB's tools for power system analysis. Ensure that the grid can handle variations in demand and supply.
7. **Visualization and Reporting**: Create visualizations and reports using MATLAB to convey the results and insights to stakeholders effectively.

```
% Sample MATLAB code for smart grid optimization

% Data acquisition

sensorData = acquireSensorData('sensor1.csv');

% Load forecasting (using LSTM neural network)

loadForecastModel = trainLoadForecastModel(sensorData);

predictedLoad = forecastLoad(loadForecastModel, futureTime);

% Renewable energy integration (modeling solar power)

solarPanelModel = createSolarPanelModel('solar_data.csv');

solarGeneration = simulateSolarGeneration(solarPanelModel,
weatherData);

% Energy storage optimization

batteryModel = designBatteryModel();
```

```
optimizedControl = optimizeBatteryControl(batteryModel, loadProfile);

% Grid control and management

gridController = createGridController();

gridStatus = simulateGridOperation(gridController, predictedLoad, solarGeneration);

% Stability analysis (power flow analysis)

powerFlowAnalysis(gridStatus);

% Visualization and reporting

plotResults(predictedLoad, solarGeneration, gridStatus);

generateReports('smart_grid_report.pdf');
```

Benefits

UTILIZING MATLAB FOR smart grid energy analysis and optimization offers several benefits:

- **Integration**: MATLAB provides a unified platform for modeling, simulation, and optimization of smart grid components.
- **Flexibility**: Custom algorithms and control strategies can be easily implemented and tested.
- **Interdisciplinary Approach**: MATLAB allows engineers, data scientists, and domain experts to collaborate on smart grid projects.

- **Visualization**: MATLAB's plotting and visualization capabilities aid in presenting insights to stakeholders.

Conclusion

THIS CASE STUDY DEMONSTRATES the application of MATLAB in analyzing and optimizing a smart grid's operation. MATLAB's versatility and extensive toolbox support make it a valuable tool for addressing the complex challenges of modern energy systems. By using MATLAB, teams can make informed decisions to enhance the efficiency, reliability, and sustainability of smart grids.

Chapter 19: Best Practices and Tips for MATLAB Users

Section 19.1: Effective Coding Practices

IN THIS SECTION, WE will discuss essential coding practices and tips for MATLAB users to write clean, efficient, and maintainable code. Adhering to these practices not only makes your code more readable but also helps avoid common pitfalls and optimize performance.

1. **Meaningful Variable Names**: Use descriptive variable names that convey the purpose of the variable. This improves code readability and understanding. For example, use temperature_data instead of temp for storing temperature data.
2. **Commenting**: Add comments to explain complex logic, algorithms, or the purpose of specific code blocks. Use MATLAB's % symbol for single-line comments and %{ ... %} for multi-line comments.

3. **Modularization**: Break your code into functions and scripts to promote code reusability. Each function should have a single, well-defined purpose.
4. **Indentation and Formatting**: Follow consistent indentation and formatting styles. MATLAB's built-in mlint tool can help identify formatting issues.
5. **Error Handling**: Implement proper error handling using try-catch blocks to handle exceptions gracefully and provide informative error messages to users.
6. **Avoid Global Variables**: Minimize the use of global variables as they can lead to unexpected side effects and make code harder to debug and maintain.
7. **Vectorization**: Leverage MATLAB's vectorization capabilities for numerical operations. Avoid unnecessary loops when working with arrays, as vectorized code is typically faster.
8. **Memory Management**: Be mindful of memory usage, especially for large datasets. Clear variables and release memory using clear or clearvars when they are no longer needed.
9. **Preallocation**: When working with arrays in loops, preallocate arrays to their final size before populating them. This avoids reallocation and improves performance.
10. **Profile Code**: Use MATLAB's built-in profiler (profile on) to identify performance bottlenecks in your code. Optimize the slowest parts of your code for better efficiency.
11. **Version Control**: Use version control systems like Git to track changes in your code, collaborate with others, and maintain a history of your project.
12. **Unit Testing**: Implement unit tests for critical parts of your code using MATLAB's testing framework. This helps

ensure that changes to your code do not introduce new bugs.

13. **Documentation**: Maintain clear and up-to-date documentation for your code, including function headers, input/output descriptions, and usage examples. This aids users and future maintainers.
14. **Code Reviews**: Consider peer code reviews to get feedback on your code's quality, readability, and correctness.
15. **MATLAB Online Resources**: Explore MATLAB's official documentation, user community forums, and online resources to stay updated with best practices and solutions to common problems.

By following these best practices, you can enhance your MATLAB coding skills, produce more reliable code, and collaborate effectively with other MATLAB users. Clean and well-documented code is not only easier to work with but also a valuable asset for your projects and research.

Section 19.2: Documentation and Code Sharing

EFFECTIVE DOCUMENTATION and code sharing are essential aspects of MATLAB development. They enable collaboration, make your code more accessible to others, and help you understand and maintain your code in the future. In this section, we'll discuss best practices for documenting your MATLAB code and sharing it with others.

1. Function Headers and Comments

• For every function you write, include a header comment that describes the function's purpose, input parameters, and output values. This helps users understand how to use your function without inspecting the code.

```
% Calculate the mean value of an array.

% Input:

% data: Input array.

% Output:

% mean_value: Mean value of the input data.

function mean_value = calculate_mean(data)

% Code implementation here

end
```

• Use inline comments to explain complex or non-intuitive parts of your code. These comments clarify your code's logic.

2. Usage Examples

• Include usage examples in your function headers or create separate script files with examples that demonstrate how to use your functions.

```
% Example usage of the calculate_mean function
```

```
data = [1, 2, 3, 4, 5];

mean_value = calculate_mean(data);

fprintf('Mean value: %f\n', mean_value);
```

3. MATLAB Publishing

• MATLAB provides the ability to create and share documents that combine code, formatted text, and visualizations using MATLAB Publishing. It's a powerful tool for creating interactive documents and tutorials.

4. GitHub and Version Control

• Use version control systems like Git and platforms like GitHub to track changes in your code, collaborate with others, and maintain a history of your project. GitHub allows you to share your code with a global community.

5. ReadMe Files

• Create a ReadMe file for your project or repository. A good ReadMe provides an overview of your project, installation instructions, usage examples, and links to documentation.

6. Documentation Generators

• Consider using documentation generators like Doxygen, Sphinx, or MATLAB's built-in publishing tools to automatically generate documentation from comments in your code.

7. Online Platforms and Forums

- Share your code and ask for help or feedback on platforms like MATLAB Central, Stack Overflow, or relevant discipline-specific forums. Engaging with the community can help you improve your code.

8. Licensing and Permissions

- Specify the licensing terms for your code. MATLAB allows you to include a license in your code to define how others can use and share it.

9. Collaboration and Contribution Guidelines

- If you're open to collaboration or contributions from others, clearly define guidelines for how others can contribute to your project.

10. Update and Maintain

- Regularly update and maintain your code and documentation as your project evolves or as issues are reported by users.

EFFECTIVE DOCUMENTATION and code sharing not only benefit others but also enhance your own development process. They make it easier to revisit and extend your code in the future, ensuring its longevity and usefulness.

Section 19.3: Community and Online Resources

ENGAGING WITH THE MATLAB community and utilizing online resources can significantly enhance your MATLAB development experience. In this section, we'll explore various ways to tap into the wealth of knowledge and support available online.

1. MATLAB Central

MATLAB CENTRAL IS MATLAB'S official online community. It's a hub for MATLAB users, developers, and MathWorks experts. You can visit MATLAB Central to:

- **Ask Questions**: Post your MATLAB-related questions in the MATLAB Answers forum, and the community or MathWorks staff can provide answers and solutions.

- **Participate in Discussions**: Join discussions on various MATLAB-related topics, from programming to toolboxes and applications.

- **Find Solutions**: Search the vast database of previously answered questions and discussions to find solutions to common problems.

- **Access Blogs and Webinars**: Explore MATLAB-related blogs and webinars to stay updated on best practices and new features.

2. Stack Overflow

STACK OVERFLOW IS A popular platform for asking technical questions and getting answers from the developer community.

MATLAB has an active presence on Stack Overflow, making it a valuable resource for troubleshooting issues and seeking advice.

When asking questions on Stack Overflow, be sure to include the "matlab" tag to attract experts in the MATLAB domain.

3. GitHub

GITHUB HOSTS A WIDE range of MATLAB projects, libraries, and repositories. You can find open-source MATLAB code, contribute to existing projects, or share your own work. GitHub is an excellent platform for collaboration and version control.

4. MATLAB Documentation and Tutorials

MATHWORKS PROVIDES comprehensive documentation for MATLAB, including user guides, function reference, and tutorials. The official documentation is a reliable source of information on MATLAB's capabilities and usage.

5. Online Courses and MOOCs

THERE ARE NUMEROUS online courses and Massive Open Online Courses (MOOCs) that teach MATLAB programming and its applications. Platforms like Coursera, edX, and Udemy offer MATLAB courses.

6. YouTube Tutorials

YOUTUBE HOSTS A VAST collection of video tutorials on MATLAB programming, ranging from beginner to advanced topics. Watching video tutorials can be a helpful way to learn and visualize concepts.

7. LinkedIn Groups

LINKEDIN HAS PROFESSIONAL groups dedicated to MATLAB users and developers. Joining these groups can connect you with like-minded professionals and provide opportunities for networking and knowledge sharing.

8. Research Papers and Journals

EXPLORE RESEARCH PAPERS and journals related to your field of interest. Many researchers share MATLAB code and algorithms in their publications, which can be a valuable resource for your own work.

9. Contribute to Open Source

CONSIDER CONTRIBUTING to open-source MATLAB projects. Collaborating on open-source projects can improve your skills and expand your network.

10. MathWorks Support

IF YOU HAVE A MATHWORKS support subscription, you can directly contact MathWorks support for technical assistance and guidance.

By actively participating in the MATLAB community and leveraging online resources, you can access a wealth of knowledge, find solutions to challenges, and enhance your proficiency in MATLAB programming and its applications. It's a valuable ecosystem for both beginners and experienced users.

Section 19.4: Career Opportunities and MATLAB Certification

MATLAB PROFICIENCY can open doors to various career opportunities in fields such as engineering, data analysis, scientific research, finance, and more. In this section, we'll explore how mastering MATLAB can benefit your career and the importance of MATLAB certification.

Career Opportunities

1. **Engineering Roles**: MATLAB is extensively used in engineering disciplines, including electrical, mechanical, aerospace, and civil engineering. Proficiency in MATLAB is often a requirement for engineering positions, especially those involving modeling, simulation, and data analysis.
2. **Data Analysis and Data Science**: MATLAB's data analysis and visualization capabilities make it valuable in data science roles. Employers in industries like finance, healthcare, and marketing seek professionals who can use MATLAB for data analysis and machine learning.
3. **Scientific Research**: MATLAB is a powerful tool for scientific research across various domains, including physics, chemistry, biology, and environmental science. Research institutions often prefer candidates with MATLAB skills for data analysis and simulation tasks.
4. **Academia**: MATLAB proficiency is advantageous for educators, as it's widely used in teaching and research at universities and academic institutions. It enables you to create educational content and conduct research efficiently.
5. **Finance and Quantitative Analysis**: In the finance industry, MATLAB is employed for risk assessment, algorithmic trading, and financial modeling. Knowledge of

MATLAB can be a significant asset in finance-related roles.

6. **Consulting and Freelancing**: MATLAB experts can work as consultants or freelancers, offering their expertise to clients across various industries. This provides flexibility and the opportunity to work on diverse projects.

MATLAB Certification

OBTAINING MATLAB CERTIFICATION is a valuable way to validate your skills and enhance your credibility as a MATLAB professional. MathWorks offers certification exams for different skill levels:

1. **MATLAB Certified Associate**: This entry-level certification demonstrates your foundational MATLAB skills, including programming fundamentals and basic data analysis.
2. **MATLAB Certified Professional**: This intermediate-level certification focuses on more advanced MATLAB concepts, including data analysis, visualization, and solving engineering and scientific problems.
3. **MATLAB Certified Expert**: The highest level of certification, MATLAB Certified Expert, recognizes your advanced proficiency in MATLAB, including developing complex applications and solving intricate problems.

Benefits of MATLAB certification:

- **Career Advancement**: Certification can open doors to better job opportunities and career growth.

- **Credibility**: It provides evidence of your MATLAB skills to potential employers or clients.

- **Personal Growth**: Preparing for the certification exams can deepen your understanding of MATLAB and expand your skill set.

- **Recognition**: MathWorks acknowledges certified professionals on their website, which can boost your visibility in the job market.

- **Competitive Edge**: In competitive job markets, certification can give you an advantage over other candidates.

- **Professional Network**: Certified professionals often join a community of like-minded individuals, fostering networking opportunities.

To prepare for MATLAB certification exams, MathWorks provides official study materials and practice tests. Whether you're a student, a professional looking to advance your career, or someone seeking freelance opportunities, MATLAB certification can be a valuable investment in your future.

Section 19.5: Continuing Education and Learning Paths

IN THE DYNAMIC FIELD of MATLAB and computational sciences, continuous learning is essential to stay up-to-date and excel in your chosen domain. In this section, we'll explore the significance of continuing education and provide insights into various learning paths you can pursue to enhance your MATLAB skills.

The Importance of Continuing Education

1. **Keeping Pace with Advancements**: Technology evolves rapidly, and MATLAB is no exception. Continuing education ensures you stay informed about the latest features, updates, and best practices in MATLAB programming.
2. **Enhancing Skill Set**: Learning doesn't stop after acquiring the basics. By pursuing advanced courses and certifications, you can diversify your skill set, making you more valuable in the job market.
3. **Meeting Industry Demands**: Different industries have specific MATLAB requirements. Ongoing education helps you align your skills with industry demands, increasing your employability.
4. **Career Growth**: Many employers value professionals who invest in their education. It can lead to promotions, salary increases, and access to more challenging and rewarding roles.
5. **Networking**: Educational programs often provide opportunities to connect with peers, mentors, and experts in the field, expanding your professional network.

MATLAB Learning Paths

TO SUPPORT YOUR ONGOING education in MATLAB, MathWorks offers structured learning paths and resources. Here are some recommended learning paths:

1. **MATLAB Fundamentals**: If you're new to MATLAB, start with the fundamentals. Learn MATLAB's basic syntax, data types, and programming concepts. MathWorks offers introductory courses and tutorials for beginners.

2. **Advanced MATLAB Programming**: Once you have a strong foundation, explore more advanced programming techniques. Topics may include object-oriented programming, optimization, and parallel computing.
3. **Data Analysis and Machine Learning**: MATLAB is powerful for data analysis and machine learning. Dive into courses that cover data preprocessing, statistical analysis, and machine learning algorithms.
4. **Signal and Image Processing**: If you're interested in signal processing or image analysis, focus on courses related to these areas. MATLAB's toolboxes offer specialized functions and tools for these domains.
5. **Simulink and Model-Based Design**: If you're working on control systems, modeling, or simulation, consider learning Simulink—a powerful tool for model-based design. MathWorks provides extensive resources for Simulink users.
6. **Domain-Specific Applications**: Depending on your field (e.g., engineering, finance, biology), explore MATLAB's applications in your domain. MathWorks offers specialized courses and toolboxes tailored to specific industries.
7. **MATLAB Certification**: Consider pursuing MATLAB certification to validate your skills. MathWorks provides certification exams at different levels, including Associate, Professional, and Expert.
8. **Online Communities and Forums**: Engage with the MATLAB community through online forums and discussion boards. Participating in discussions and asking questions can enhance your problem-solving skills.
9. **MathWorks Documentation**: MathWorks provides comprehensive documentation for MATLAB and its toolboxes. Regularly refer to official documentation for

reference and to discover new features.

10. **Collaborative Projects**: Collaborating on projects with peers or contributing to open-source MATLAB projects can be a hands-on way to apply your skills and learn from others.

Remember that learning is a continuous journey, and there's always something new to discover in MATLAB. Regularly update your knowledge to adapt to changing industry trends and keep your skills sharp. By investing in your education, you can unlock new opportunities and achieve greater success in your MATLAB-related endeavors.

Chapter 20: The Future of MATLAB

Section 20.1: Emerging Trends in MATLAB Programming

THE WORLD OF PROGRAMMING and computational sciences is ever-evolving, and MATLAB is no exception. In this section, we'll explore some of the emerging trends and developments in MATLAB programming that are shaping the future of this versatile tool.

1. Interoperability with Other Languages

AS THE COMPUTATIONAL landscape becomes more diverse, the need for interoperability between programming languages is growing. MATLAB is increasingly focusing on seamless integration with languages like Python, Julia, and R. This allows users to harness the strengths of multiple languages within a single workflow.

2. Enhanced AI and Machine Learning Capabilities

MACHINE LEARNING AND artificial intelligence are at the forefront of technological advancements. MATLAB continues to enhance its capabilities in these domains, offering improved support for deep learning, reinforcement learning, and natural language processing. The integration of pre-trained models and automation of machine learning workflows simplifies complex tasks.

3. Cloud Integration and Scalability

CLOUD COMPUTING IS changing the way we handle data and computations. MATLAB is adapting to this trend by offering cloud integration, enabling users to access cloud resources seamlessly. This not only facilitates scalability but also allows for collaborative work and remote access to MATLAB environments.

4. GPU Acceleration and High-Performance Computing

WITH THE INCREASING availability of powerful GPUs, MATLAB is focusing on optimizing GPU acceleration for computationally intensive tasks. High-performance computing (HPC) capabilities are also being enhanced to harness the full potential of modern hardware.

5. Explainable AI and Ethical Considerations

ETHICAL CONCERNS AND transparency in AI are gaining importance. MATLAB is incorporating tools and features that facilitate the interpretation of machine learning models, making it easier to understand and explain their decisions. This is crucial for ensuring the ethical use of AI in various applications.

6. Integration with IoT and Sensor Data

THE INTERNET OF THINGS (IoT) is generating vast amounts of sensor data. MATLAB is adapting to this data-rich environment by offering tools for seamless integration with IoT devices, enabling real-time data analysis, predictive maintenance, and more.

7. Advancements in Simulink

SIMULINK, MATLAB'S companion for model-based design, is also evolving. It now offers improved support for autonomous systems, robotics, and control engineering. Users can simulate complex systems more efficiently, making it a valuable tool for various industries.

8. Sustainability and Green Technologies

AS SUSTAINABILITY BECOMES a global priority, MATLAB is being employed in environmental modeling, renewable energy, and sustainable technology development. Researchers and engineers are using MATLAB to tackle challenges related to climate change and resource conservation.

9. Education and Accessibility

MATLAB IS COMMITTED to improving accessibility and educational resources. It offers various initiatives and programs to support learning and research in academic institutions, ensuring that the next generation of scientists and engineers have access to the tools they need.

10. Community Collaboration and Open Source

COMMUNITY ENGAGEMENT and collaboration are vital in shaping the future of MATLAB. Initiatives like MATLAB Central and File Exchange promote the sharing of knowledge and open-source contributions, fostering a vibrant ecosystem of MATLAB users.

In conclusion, MATLAB's future is marked by adaptability and innovation. It continues to evolve to meet the changing needs of researchers, engineers, and data scientists across various domains. By staying at the forefront of emerging trends, MATLAB remains a powerful and indispensable tool in the world of computational sciences and engineering.

Section 20.2: Future of Computational Sciences with MATLAB

IN THE EVER-EVOLVING landscape of computational sciences, MATLAB continues to play a pivotal role in shaping the future. In this section, we will delve into some of the key areas where MATLAB is anticipated to make significant contributions and innovations.

1. Multidisciplinary Research

INTERDISCIPLINARY RESEARCH is becoming increasingly prevalent in fields such as biology, physics, and engineering. MATLAB's versatility allows researchers from different domains to collaborate seamlessly. The future holds even more promise for interdisciplinary research as MATLAB expands its capabilities and toolboxes.

2. Quantum Computing

QUANTUM COMPUTING IS on the horizon, and MATLAB is keeping pace with this disruptive technology. Researchers can leverage MATLAB to simulate quantum algorithms, develop quantum-inspired optimization techniques, and explore quantum machine learning. As quantum computing matures, MATLAB will continue to provide essential tools for this emerging field.

3. Computational Chemistry and Materials Science

ADVANCEMENTS IN COMPUTATIONAL chemistry and materials science are critical for innovations in materials design, drug discovery, and clean energy. MATLAB is expected to play a crucial role in simulating molecular structures, predicting chemical reactions, and optimizing materials for various applications.

4. Climate Modeling and Environmental Studies

CLIMATE CHANGE MITIGATION and environmental sustainability are pressing global challenges. MATLAB's capabilities in modeling complex systems will be instrumental in climate modeling, ecosystem analysis, and environmental impact assessments. Researchers can utilize MATLAB to develop models for predicting climate patterns and evaluating the effectiveness of environmental policies.

5. Personalized Medicine

THE FIELD OF HEALTHCARE is moving towards personalized medicine, where treatments are tailored to individual patients. MATLAB's data analytics and machine learning capabilities will be essential in analyzing vast amounts of patient data, identifying genetic markers, and optimizing treatment plans based on individual genetic profiles.

6. Space Exploration and Astronomy

MATLAB HAS A LONG HISTORY of involvement in space exploration and astronomy. With the growing interest in space travel and exploration, MATLAB will continue to be used for mission planning, data analysis from space telescopes, and simulations of celestial phenomena. Its role in space research is expected to expand further.

7. Cybersecurity and Data Privacy

AS CYBERSECURITY THREATS become more sophisticated, MATLAB's capabilities in data analysis and anomaly detection will be crucial for identifying and mitigating security breaches.

Additionally, MATLAB can be used to develop encryption and data privacy solutions to protect sensitive information.

8. Fusion of AI and Scientific Computing

THE SYNERGY BETWEEN artificial intelligence (AI) and scientific computing is a game-changer. MATLAB's integration of AI capabilities with scientific computing will lead to more efficient data analysis, predictive modeling, and automation of research tasks.

9. Human-Machine Collaboration

THE FUTURE WILL WITNESS increased collaboration between humans and machines. MATLAB's development of human-readable, interpretable AI models will facilitate collaboration and trust-building between researchers and AI algorithms.

10. Educational Advancements

MATLAB WILL CONTINUE to be a cornerstone of education in scientific and engineering disciplines. It will adapt to the evolving needs of educators and students, providing accessible and interactive tools for teaching and learning.

In conclusion, MATLAB's future in computational sciences is marked by its adaptability, innovation, and continued relevance across a broad spectrum of fields. As emerging technologies and research areas evolve, MATLAB is well-positioned to empower researchers, scientists, and engineers in their quest for knowledge and solutions to complex challenges.

Section 20.3: MATLAB in Space Exploration and Astronomy

SPACE EXPLORATION AND astronomy have always been at the forefront of scientific discovery, capturing the human imagination and driving technological advancements. MATLAB plays a vital role in these fields, providing researchers and engineers with the tools necessary to explore the cosmos, analyze astronomical data, and simulate celestial phenomena.

1. Mission Planning and Navigation

MATLAB IS USED EXTENSIVELY in mission planning for space exploration. It aids in trajectory calculations, orbital mechanics, and navigation for spacecraft. Engineers can simulate different mission scenarios, optimize trajectories, and ensure safe navigation through complex space environments.

```
% Example of orbital trajectory calculation

initialConditions = [7000, 0, 0, 0, 7.67, 0];

options = odeset('RelTol', 1e-8);

[t, state] = ode45(@orbitalEquations, [0, 10000], initialConditions, options);

function dydt = orbitalEquations(~, state)

% Define differential equations for orbital motion

% ...

dydt = [state(4); state(5); state(6); ...];

end
```

2. Data Analysis and Image Processing

ASTRONOMERS RELY ON MATLAB for data analysis and image processing. MATLAB's image processing toolbox offers powerful algorithms for enhancing, filtering, and segmenting astronomical images. Additionally, it enables researchers to extract valuable information from large datasets produced by space telescopes.

```
% Example of image processing for star detection

image = imread('telescope_image.jpg');

filteredImage = imfilter(image, gaussianFilter);

binaryImage = imbinarize(filteredImage, threshold);

starProperties = regionprops(binaryImage, 'Centroid', 'Area');
```

3. Simulating Celestial Phenomena

MATLAB IS USED TO SIMULATE and model celestial phenomena, such as planetary motion, solar system dynamics, and gravitational interactions. Researchers can create accurate simulations to study the behavior of celestial bodies and understand cosmic events.

```
% Example of simulating planetary motion

G = 6.67430e-11; % Gravitational constant (m^3/kg/s^2)

massSun = 1.989e30; % Mass of the Sun (kg)

massEarth = 5.972e24; % Mass of the Earth (kg)

initialPosition = [147e9, 0]; % Initial position of Earth from the Sun (m)
```

```
initialVelocity = [0, 29784]; % Initial velocity of Earth (m/s)

% Calculate Earth's trajectory using numerical integration

[t, position] = ode45(@(t, y) gravitationalEquations(t, y, G, massSun), [0, 365*24*3600], [initialPosition, initialVelocity]);

function dydt = gravitationalEquations(~, y, G, massSun)

% Define differential equations for gravitational motion

r = norm(y(1:2));

dydt = [y(3); y(4); -G * massSun / r^3 * y(1); -G * massSun / r^3 * y(2)];

end
```

4. Telescope Control and Automation

MODERN OBSERVATORIES and telescopes often rely on MATLAB for control and automation. MATLAB interfaces with telescope systems, enabling astronomers to point telescopes accurately, capture images, and conduct observations remotely. Automation allows for more efficient data collection.

```
% Example of telescope control commands

telescope = TelescopeController('COM3');

telescope.connect();

telescope.moveToCoordinates(celestialCoordinates);

image = telescope.captureImage();

telescope.disconnect();
```

5. Gravitational Wave Analysis

THE DETECTION OF GRAVITATIONAL waves has opened new frontiers in astrophysics. MATLAB is used to analyze and process data from gravitational wave detectors, such as LIGO and Virgo. Researchers can extract valuable information from gravitational wave signals, leading to discoveries related to black holes, neutron stars, and the fabric of spacetime.

In conclusion, MATLAB's contributions to space exploration and astronomy are vast and multidimensional. Whether it's simulating the motion of celestial bodies, processing astronomical images, or analyzing complex datasets, MATLAB continues to empower researchers and scientists in their quest to unravel the mysteries of the universe. As technology advances and our understanding of the cosmos deepens, MATLAB will remain an indispensable tool in these captivating fields.

Section 20.4: The Role of MATLAB in Sustainable Technologies

SUSTAINABLE TECHNOLOGIES have gained significant importance in recent years as we address the challenges of climate change and environmental conservation. MATLAB plays a crucial role in advancing sustainable technologies by providing tools for modeling, simulation, and optimization in various domains. Here, we explore how MATLAB contributes to sustainability in energy, transportation, agriculture, and more.

1. Renewable Energy Systems

MATLAB IS WIDELY USED to model and optimize renewable energy systems such as solar, wind, and hydropower. Engineers and researchers can simulate the performance of solar panels, wind turbines, and energy storage systems under different conditions. This helps in designing efficient and sustainable energy solutions.

```
% Example of solar panel performance simulation

solarPanel = SolarPanelModel('panel_specifications.xml');

weatherData = load('weather_data.mat');

simulationResults = solarPanel.simulatePerformance(weatherData);
```

2. Electric Vehicle (EV) Development

IN THE TRANSPORTATION sector, MATLAB plays a vital role in the development of electric vehicles (EVs). Engineers use MATLAB to model EV components, design battery management systems, and optimize energy efficiency. This contributes to reducing greenhouse gas emissions and promoting sustainable transportation.

```
% Example of battery pack modeling for an electric vehicle

batteryPack = BatteryPackModel('pack_specifications.xml');

driveCycleData = load('drive_cycle_data.mat');

simulationResults =
batteryPack.simulatePerformance(driveCycleData);
```

3. Sustainable Agriculture

AGRICULTURE IS ANOTHER area where MATLAB's capabilities are leveraged for sustainability. Researchers use MATLAB to model crop growth, analyze soil data, and optimize irrigation systems. This helps in reducing water usage, enhancing crop yield, and minimizing environmental impact.

```
% Example of crop growth modeling and optimization
```

```
cropModel = CropGrowthModel('crop_parameters.xml');

soilData = load('soil_data.mat');

optimizationResults = cropModel.optimizeIrrigation(soilData);
```

4. Environmental Monitoring

MATLAB IS EMPLOYED in environmental monitoring projects to process and analyze data from various sensors and remote sensing platforms. It aids in assessing air and water quality, monitoring deforestation, and studying biodiversity. These applications contribute to informed decision-making for environmental conservation.

```
% Example of air quality data analysis

airQualityData = load('air_quality_data.mat');

analysisResults = analyzeAirQualityData(airQualityData);
```

5. Sustainable Building Design

ARCHITECTS AND ENGINEERS use MATLAB for sustainable building design. It helps in modeling building energy consumption, optimizing HVAC systems, and evaluating the environmental impact of construction materials. Sustainable building practices reduce energy consumption and greenhouse gas emissions.

```
% Example of building energy simulation

buildingModel = BuildingEnergyModel('building_specifications.xml');

simulationResults = buildingModel.simulateEnergyUsage();
```

In summary, MATLAB plays a pivotal role in promoting sustainable technologies across various sectors. Its capabilities in modeling, simulation, and optimization contribute to the development of efficient and environmentally friendly solutions. As the world continues to prioritize sustainability, MATLAB will remain a valuable tool in the hands of researchers and engineers working towards a greener and more sustainable future.

Section 20.5: MATLAB and the Advancement of AI and Machine Learning

ARTIFICIAL INTELLIGENCE (AI) and Machine Learning (ML) have witnessed significant advancements, and MATLAB has played a crucial role in accelerating this progress. In this section, we delve into how MATLAB contributes to the development and deployment of AI and ML models, making it an indispensable tool for researchers, engineers, and data scientists.

1. Deep Learning Frameworks

MATLAB PROVIDES SUPPORT for popular deep learning frameworks, including TensorFlow, PyTorch, and Keras. This integration allows users to leverage pre-trained models, build custom architectures, and perform transfer learning seamlessly.

```
% Example of using a pre-trained deep learning model

net = importKerasNetwork('my_model.h5');

image = imread('test_image.jpg');

predictions = predict(net, image);
```

2. Data Preparation and Preprocessing

EFFECTIVE DATA PREPARATION is critical in ML projects. MATLAB offers a wide range of tools for data preprocessing, including data cleaning, feature selection, and dimensionality reduction. This ensures that data is ready for training and testing ML models.

```
% Example of data preprocessing
data = readtable('raw_data.csv');
cleanedData = preprocessData(data);
```

3. Machine Learning Model Development

MATLAB PROVIDES A COMPREHENSIVE environment for developing ML models. Users can create classification, regression, clustering, and reinforcement learning models with ease. The availability of built-in algorithms simplifies the model development process.

```
% Example of training a support vector machine (SVM) classifier
svmModel = fitcsvm(trainingData, labels);
```

4. Explainable AI and Interpretability

INTERPRETING ML MODEL predictions is essential for building trust in AI systems. MATLAB offers tools for model interpretability, allowing users to understand feature importance, generate explanations, and identify potential biases.

```
% Example of generating feature importance scores
```

importanceScores = calculateFeatureImportance(trainedModel, testData);

5. Deployment and Integration

MATLAB ENABLES THE deployment of AI and ML models to various platforms, including embedded devices and cloud services. Integration with external systems and APIs is straightforward, making it possible to deploy models in real-world applications.

% Example of deploying an ML model as a RESTful API

deployedModel = deployModelAsAPI(trainedModel);

6. AutoML and Hyperparameter Tuning

AUTOML CAPABILITIES in MATLAB automate the process of selecting the best ML algorithms and hyperparameters. This accelerates model development and reduces the need for manual tuning.

% Example of using AutoML to optimize model hyperparameters

bestModel = autoMLTuneHyperparameters(trainingData, labels);

7. Research and Innovation

RESEARCHERS BENEFIT from MATLAB's extensibility and ability to experiment with cutting-edge AI and ML techniques. It serves as a platform for developing novel algorithms and conducting research in AI-related fields.

% Example of developing a novel deep learning architecture

customNet = createCustomDeepLearningModel();

In conclusion, MATLAB empowers the AI and ML community by providing a comprehensive ecosystem for model development, training, deployment, and research. Its versatility and integration with popular frameworks make it a go-to choice for those pushing the boundaries of AI and ML technologies. As AI continues to transform industries and society, MATLAB remains at the forefront, enabling innovation and progress in this dynamic field.

www.ingramcontent.com/pod-product-compliance
Lightning Source LLC
LaVergne TN
LVHW090303210926
848480LV00001B/118
* 9 7 9 8 2 2 4 6 7 1 7 4 8 *